Credit Risk Management
The Novel

Part One

A chronicle of one man's efforts to bring Peace to the World, and his Team's determination to provide added value, future orientated, credit management solutions, despite his frequent inattention.

Featuring Office of Peace Secret Agent & Credit Executive James E. Cricket and his dedicated Credit Team

AUTHOR: RON WELLS

PUBLISHED BY: T3P LIMITED

Printed by CreateSpace, an Amazon.com Company

Available from Amazon.com and other retail outlets

Published by: T3P LIMITED
Registered in England & Wales   Co. Number: 4344371
First Floor MIDAS House   Tel: +44 20 8123 0139
62 Goldsworth Road   Email: info@t3plimited.com
Woking Surrey GU21 6LQ   URL: www.t3plimited.com
United Kingdom

Author: Ron Wells

ISBN: 978-0-9576279-2-5

RON WELLS

Preface

Welcome to the first narrative non-fiction novel to feature the true to life experiences of a team of professionals managing business to business credit risk, day to day. This creative and personally satisfying endeavour is set within the context of the largely untold story of the inexorable progress the human race is making towards achieving world peace.

Those who seek to give world peace a positive boost from time to time, like our wannabe-hero James E Cricket and the Office of Peace must tread carefully. They must avoid attracting the wrath of those who have a vested interest in maintaining, even increasing the fear, hatred, distrust and avarice between people and nations, which are the foundation stones of war.

James conceals his endeavours on behalf of peace by managing the credit risk for a global enterprise. In so doing he and his colleague Jenny pass on their accumulated experience and knowledge to fellow team members and to you the reader.

In business to business credit management we do not lend money, rather we trust people. You cannot trust someone you do not know, so corporate credit executives must first come to know their counterparties. They do this by means of research, analysis, assessment and human interaction, within the context of the market and with a considered view of the future.

The media bombard us with crime and violence only because our instinct is to highlight danger to be avoided, so such reports are certain to gain our attention. Hence the good things that occur largely go unnoticed, but more good things than bad things must be happening, or humanity would not still exist.

As global citizens we should all enjoy peace, prosperity and freedom, all seven billion plus of us.

Credit energises the markets that create and sustain prosperity.

Ron Wells
Passionate believer in the value of Purpose Driven
Creative Credit Management

Part One

Chapter 1

Berlin & Washington DC 1989 November

Jim employs his considerable negotiating skills with a Soviet General and the President of the USA, to ensure the Berlin Wall is dismantled peacefully.

Chapter 2

London 1989 December

Jim plans to meet with FW de Klerk, the President of South Africa, in Dublin. He also helps Jenny to prepare to deliver her début credit conference presentation, in case she has to replace him.

Chapter 3

London 1990 January

Jim prepares for the meeting with FW de Klerk, and helps Wei Ming (the Collateral Manager) to deal with a sticky situation involving a Letter of Credit confirmation and a tight deadline.

Chapter 4

Dublin 1990 January

Jim lands in Dublin, does some sightseeing and finalises his preparations for the important meeting. Jenny steps in to make the conference presentation prepared for Jim, while he meets with 'FW de Klerk'. Jim's meeting is bizarre and unproductive, but he draws solace from the fact that Jenny's début is a triumph.

Chapter 5

London 1990 February

Jim lunches with an old friend, Roger (French pronunciation) Dreyfus. Jenny shares her presentation and what she learnt at the conference with Jim and Wei Ming.
FW de Klerk dismantles apartheid in his opening speech to Parliament; peace in South Africa takes a giant step forward.

Chapter 6

London 1990 February

Jim celebrates Nelson Mandela's release and receives a request from his boss, Oleg (Oily) Solovyov, to prepare to assist Gorbachev in his efforts to reform the Soviet Union peacefully. Oily foresees the breakup of the Soviet Union providing opportunities for ShamOil to become involved in crude oil production in the Central Asian States.
Wei Ming learns how to deal with an Import Letter of Credit request received from a small trading house.

Chapter 7

London 1990 February

Jim is alerted to the formation of the Two plus Four Ministerial group to negotiate the reunification of Germany, and subsequent consolidation of European peace. He is asked to stand ready to help keep the negotiations on track should any hurdles appear.

Jim recalls his visit to Czechoslovakia during the Prague Spring. In August Jim and fellow university student Roger arrive in Prague, to spend ten days as guests of Jim's Uncle Gerald. Gerald is an employee of the UK Foreign Office stationed at the British Embassy. He provides an introduction to the local political scene and arranges for two local students to host his guests over the weekend.

Chapter 8

Prague 1968 August

Their hosts introduce Jim and Roger to fellow students over lunch, and they take in the major tourist sites; Castle District, Charles Bridge, Old Town Square and an historic Synagogue. In the evening they visit a jazz club and Jim meets an enigmatic local character, Josef Koudelka.

Chapter 9

Prague 1968 August

Four days into their visit Gerald summons Jim and Roger to the Embassy, where they sense tension in the air. Gerald's concerns are vindicated when Soviet forces invade Czechoslovakia. Subsequently Jim and Roger play a vital role in ensuring that people in the 'Free World' can appreciate the agony, revulsion, solidarity and cry for freedom of the people of Czechoslovakia, through the medium of dramatic photographs taken during the fateful week that follows the invasion.

Chapter 10

London 1990 February

Snapped out of his musing Jim is confronted by another present day credit challenge. Fortunately Jenny has the situation well in hand; nevertheless a significant loss could result.
Jim learns of plans to export refined product to Nigeria and asks Jenny to provide him with a copy of the "Single Risk Credit Insurance" presentation that was imparted in Dublin.

Chapter 11

London 1990 June

James and Jenny visit Lloyds of London to meet with insurance broker Finlay Finlayson. They learn about the history and operations of the insurance market, and gain a good understanding of what is involved in utilising Credit and/or Political Risk Insurance to limit counterparty risk.

File 13 – a.k.a. Jim's Paper Recycle Bin

BIBLIOGRAPHY

Cast of Characters and Organisations

Fictional:

James E Cricket
General Orlov
Jenny Lindberg
Lee, Wei Ming
Oleg (Oily) Solovyov
Mike Rhodes
Danie van der Merwe
Roger Dreyfus (French pronunciation)
Simon Jones
ShamOil Supply & Trading UK Limited
Office of Peace (OoP)

Jean-Francois Piton
M le Branché
SimpleTrade Associates SA
Prasem
Willy Slater
Gerald Bond
Beda Dudik
Irena Nesvadbová
Kinia Gabor
June Green
John K
Phoenix Trading EPE
Success Trading EPE
Finlay Finlayson

Factual:

John Lennon
George H W Bush
Gary Hamel
Ian Angell
Ketan J Patel
Piet Retief
Zulu Chief Dingane
F W de Klerk
P W Botha
The National Party
Govan Mbeki
Nelson Mandela
Bishop Desmond Tutu
Oliver Tambo
Allister Sparks
Springboks (SA National rugby team)
Rapid Results College
Mikhail Sergeyevich Gorbachev
GCMG – Global Credit Management Group
Egyptian General Petroleum Co (EGPC)

Nigerian National Petroleum Corp (NNPC)
Paribas
Swiss Bank Corporation
Banque Nationale de Paris (BNP)
Société Générale
United Overseas Bank (UOB)
James Addison Baker (Secretary of State USA)
Hans-Dietrich Genscher
Eduard Ambrosis dze Shevardnadze
 (Minister of Foreign Affairs Soviet Union)
Alexander Dubcek
Ludvik Svoboda
Ludvik Vaculik
Hans Dulfer
Josef Koudelka
Platts
FCIB – Finance Credit & International Business
Lloyds of London
Zurich Global Corporate - UK

Chapter 1

Berlin & Washington DC 1989 November

Breathing heavily and shaking like a frightened kitten, Jim Cricket hugged the relative safety of a wall as he inched his way towards his next appointment. He was armed only with a flak jacket and a rather weak, but he hoped winning, smile that hardly disguised his chattering teeth. Meeting General Orlov in the middle of his Division's annual live ammunition firing exercise at the Soviet Army's range outside East Berlin was not Jim's idea of an ideal setting. He was after-all there to promote peace but as usual he was made to feel as unwelcome as a bout of common cold in summer.

Orlov was abrupt, loud and met Jim with a fixed stare, Jim summoned up the little will power he had to stare back. He was well aware that Russians judge the honesty of an individual by the ability to maintain eye contact. Fortunately Orlov was a fluent English speaker so there was no need for an interpreter. The clatter of gun-fire was enough of a communication obstacle, a 'go-between' would have made Jim's mission even more difficult.

Orlov demanded to know why Jim had the temerity to interrupt him in the midst of his important duties, and just what gave Jim the arrogant cheek to have a Chief Marshall order him to entertain an English wet-blanket. Jim's lizard brain kicked in screaming; 'Run, hide, we are in danger, run, run, run!' Jim instantly recognised the instinctive reaction of his primeval auto-pilot trying to 'protect' him from completing his mission. He would have achieved nothing in life if he had listened to the fear response and avoided taking risks for peace. Fortunately he had developed a way to put his lizard brain back in its box and give his neo-cortex a chance to rule. So as the strains of 'Give Peace a Chance' resonated in his mind, and holding Orlov's fixed stare, he took a deep breath and shouted back, 'Well sir I'm here to ask you to return to barracks and give peace a chance'.

'*Give Peace a Chance!* – what are you some sort of Lennon fan recently escaped from an asylum?' retorted Orlov. 'People are talking of massing at the wall determined to tear it down with bare hands, and where will that leave my men and me, totally exposed! Our position would be completely indefensible in barracks! Return to barracks is not an option; we pick the place and defend ourselves when the Americans start hunting!'

With that Orlov turned and strode away, disappearing in the smoke and noise of the artillery practice that opened with a volley. Jim shuddered, obviously a new tack would be required, as ever peace would be as difficult to achieve as victory in war, but always with less casualties. The thought gave him hope, now if only he could make the music stop playing in his head he might be able to work out a new strategy.

Having passed through Check Point Charlie and found a taxi, Jim was soon on his way to tiny Tegel Airport. Situated in the French sector of Berlin, Tegel was built in record time by local labour supervised by French engineers. It was urgently needed at the time, to supplement the two existing airfields during the Soviet land transport blockade of West Berlin. The blockade lasted from June 1948 until May 1949. During that time the people of the Allied controlled sectors of Berlin were supplied with food and fuel exclusively by air. The United States, British and Australian air forces supplied the aircraft, crews and technicians; the French – whose air force was then virtually non-existent - contributed by building the third airport in their sector. Road and rail transport routes to Berlin, through Soviet occupied Germany, had not been formally agreed amongst the Occupying Powers but air corridors had, so the Soviets did not have a legitimate basis on which to thwart the 'air-train'. The airlift was so successfully operated, with the involvement of thousands of Berliner volunteers, that by April 1949 it was delivering all essential supplies in quantities equivalent to those delivered by rail and road previously. The Soviet authorities subsequently lifted the blockade having realised that their attempt to force the western controlled sectors to rely on them for supplies, and thereby effectively cede control of Berlin to them, had failed.

After a relatively short flight to messy Heathrow, Jim boarded the sublime Concorde, and touched down in Washington DC just three hours after take-off. 'Concorde, what an amazing technical achievement - if only people put as much effort around making peace.' That was the thought that crossed Jim's mind as he stepped off the engineering marvel, took the diplomatic channel and headed for a taxi. 'The Whitehouse please driver!'

Thankfully, although the morning was chilly as autumn hung on, resisting winter's grip, the weather and the traffic did not impede Jim's journey. He had a 9 o'clock with the President so he shaved as the taxi sped on its way. Jim knew he needed to make a 'professional' impression when received, if he was to achieve his objective.

The Secret Service at the gatehouse were as polite as ever but not even world peace hanging in the balance would persuade them to hurry their thorough security checks. Jim tried to hide his impatience but worried that his body language would betray his anxiety and trigger the guards' instinctive alarm bells. After what seemed like 50 but was in fact less than 10 minutes of careful scrutiny, he was on his way to one of the most important meetings of his life. His transport was provided by a battery powered vehicle similar to those used on golf courses. Jim smiled as he thought 'speed of sound Concorde to pedestrian golf buggy in one day'.

The short journey to a side entrance gave Jim a welcome opportunity to relax and collect his thoughts, while his eyes drank in the iconic view of the seat of US power. Once inside he made a quick stop in the Restroom to brush his teeth, straighten his tie and comb his hair then he was ready to meet the President.

'Sir as we were told to expect, the GDR has today announced that the Berlin Wall checkpoints will be opened at midnight, and the people allowed to freely pass to and fro. It is already 3pm in Berlin and 5 pm in Moscow and people are massing on both sides of the wall. It is reported that they are 'drinking beer and champagne and chanting Tor auf! - Open the gate!'

'I met with the Soviet commander of the Division stationed in East Berlin yesterday. He is convinced that the wall will be torn down and Allied forces will attack his troops. He has repositioned his troops and artillery on the pretext of undertaking a routine live-firing exercise. In reality he is preparing defensive strategies and will certainly attack any Allied forces that might enter the Russian Sector. I'm afraid that if he receives inaccurate or misinterpreted information he may launch a pre-emptive strike. The situation could deteriorate very quickly. I tried to convince General Orlov to give peace a chance, but he is fearful for the safety of the men under his command. He finds it difficult to believe the Allies have good intentions.'

The President's reaction indicated that he understood the situation and knew what to do; he reached for the red phone. Jim watched spell-bound realising he was about to witness a defining moment in history.

'Dobriy vecher Mr Secretary I am calling to reassure you and appeal for your help'. The President spoke slowly and deliberately, avoiding ambiguity, double-negatives and confusing words like 'get' and 'set'; he paused frequently to allow the interpreter (who was also on the line) to translate, as he explained.

Within the next hour the General Secretary, having accepted the President's personal assurance that the Allies would not attack and indeed would guarantee the safety of the Soviet troops based in the GDR, ordered all such troops to return to barracks and await further instructions.

As History.com records: on November 9, 1989 "at midnight, ordinary people flooded through the checkpoints. More than two million people from East Berlin visited West Berlin that weekend to participate in a celebration that was, one journalist wrote, "the greatest street party in the history of the world." People used hammers and picks to knock away chunks of the wall–they became known as 'mauerspechte,' or 'wall woodpeckers'—while cranes and bulldozers pulled down section after section. Soon the wall was gone and Berlin was united for the first time since 1945. "Only today is the war really over" one Berliner spray-painted on a piece of the wall."

So peace broke out in a corner of the world, a modern miracle was witnessed in November 1989, something the 'experts' all predicted only after the event, something Nassim N Taleb would later call a Black Swan event, a positive Black Swan event.

Well, that is how Jim would have liked his report to his Handler to have read; recording how he played a vital role in assuring this miraculous step toward creation of world peace. If only he had not missed both vital appointments. If only the Skoda he hired in West Berlin had not broken down a kilometre from the crossing. If only he had not missed his East Berlin contact and spent the night trying to explain to border guards why a Credit Executive was carrying a flak jacket and a letter of introduction to a Russian General, without blowing his cover. Jim was convinced everything would have worked out exactly as he planned.... If only his Diplomatic Channel pass had not expired, forcing him to wait forty-five minutes in an immigration queue, he would not have been told by the President's aide, 'Sorry the President is on the phone with Moscow, he will not be able to meet you today'.

At least President George H W Bush had managed to do the right thing while Jim was in line waiting to clear Immigration Control, so all is well that ends well. Jim's day in DC was after-all otherwise well spent with visits to the National Air and Space Museum, the Capitol Building and the National Gallery of Art, creating memories for him that could last a lifetime.

Chapter 2

London 1989 December

Daydreaming about past near-victories that might have been was a stress-free way to pass the time, if slightly depressing – perhaps his next assignment would be a real success. Given his missed opportunities Jim could not bring himself to feel any sense of personal achievement as a result of the outcome of his last mission. With that he shook off the visualising and reverted to the present as his super-smart, patient and hardworking colleague, Jenny Lindberg broke the silence.

'So what do you want to talk about at the Dublin Conference, JE?' She could not bring herself to call Jim 'JC' because his ego was dangerously close to becoming over-inflated. On the other hand, although they had worked together for a year, she would only refer to him as 'Jiminy' when with close friends.

Jim was not particularly inspired by the thought of having to speak about Credit Risk Management to the GCMG crowd in Dublin, but it would give him the opportunity to add a clandestine meeting with F W de Klerk on the side. F W had recently taken over the Presidential reigns in South Africa from his tentatively reformist predecessor, P W Botha, and seemed to be determined to follow a more radical reform agenda. Jim's plan was to nudge the process forward with the offer of some sage advice and the whole hearted support of the Office of Peace.

'J!' exclaimed Jenny, noticing the glazed look in his eyes. 'Attention please, I must have your presentation sent to the conference organiser by Friday – which topics are you going to address?'

Jim smiled; he was constantly amazed at the enthusiasm with which Jenny approached the subject of credit risk management. Although he had seen similar enthusiasm displayed at gatherings of credit-philes, he surmised that that was only as a result of a combination of the alcohol imbibed by those attending and the conference organiser's choice of location. However Jenny's enthusiasm was unquestionably genuine.

'I want to wake up and engage the audience, what can you suggest as a subject that might achieve that, something controversial?' said Jim switching on to the subject at last.

'You could talk about the vital role business to business credit granting can play in fostering the survival and growth of businesses, and creating stable employment opportunities.'

'Nonsense, credit management is only about reading credit reports, plugging in credit limits according to some boring matrix, insisting on security or cash in advance for new businesses, and chasing overdue invoices. Anyone who can read a step-by-step manual can do that, no need to engage a brain. You make the job sound like it's an opportunity to make the world a better place. Everyone knows credit management's mission is to prevent sales or give as little credit as possible, then upset potential customers by hounding and threatening them when payments are overdue. Honestly when I witness your enthusiasm at the mention of the word credit I think you must take happy pills, or perhaps you are actually Alice trapped behind the looking glass!'

'Oh you are so wrong, your info' is so early 20th century, businesses that are ahead of the curve don't think or act as you describe. They understand that growing the businesses of their customers and suppliers is in their best interests. If they achieve that their own businesses automatically register healthy growth. Credit is not a zero sum game, if you play by the correct rules it's a win-win opportunity.

Coincidentally, I've made a start on a presentation to address this subject; I've even written a Purpose statement to give meaning to the work of a credit management executive. It covers how they can make the world a better place. Not everyone can spend their time promoting world peace.'

'Well you better show me this Purpose statement. I can't conceive how minimising the number of days of credit given after delivery of the goods, and minimising bad debts; that is to say stunting and inhibiting the growth of businesses helps make the world a better place? No-way!'

'You are such a sceptic! Here it is, read it and then apologise....'

Jim took the paper proffered by Jenny and read:

PURPOSE

Nourishing Businesses... The Credit Team seeks to provide credit solutions that enhance internal and external customers' and suppliers' business models and sustainability.

The foundations for this work are:
- Compliance with Credit Policy,
- Holistic credit analysis,
- A "Yes; provided .... Can Do" attitude, and
- An on-going programme of research, development, participation in professional discussions, and networking.

'Hmm that makes credit management seem useful. We need an eye-catching title. What about grabbing attention with "Cash Only – No Credit Given – No Credit Manager Required" then making the completely opposite case in the presentation?'

'That title should certainly spike the curiosity of Global Credit Management Group members! Let's stick to the content for the moment though, since we are finally starting to make some progress.'

'Okay, what about Values and a Vision Statement, have you created draft templates for aspiring credit executives yet?'

'Naturally!' retorted Jenny, producing a couple of pages with a flourish:

VALUES

Integrity, Trust, Transparency, Creativity and Enterprise

In the event of conflict between these values, Integrity takes precedence. A decision based on Integrity is one that the decider would be proud to publish and defend.

VISION

Credit Team is an innovative, market leading, customer focused credit solutions provider - fully aligned with the Company's Strategic Intent. It is recognised as having great people with imagination, committed to delivering added value to internal and external customers. The team works 'as one'; guided by the values of integrity, trust, transparency, creativity and enterprise.

'Good job! When world peace is achieved I'll definitely consider taking up the credit profession!'

'I think I'll need more on business Strategy though; you said that playing by the rules creates win-win opportunities. I assume there are strategy-based policies. When is it appropriate to invest a company's scarce working capital in financing the cash cycle of its customers?'

'That is easy; there are five good 'and/or' reasons:

Product Enhancement

Comparative Cost of Money

Administrative Efficiency

Building Trust

Business Development'

'A little more than headings will be needed.'

'Of course, here is a draft for the detail,' said Jenny as she handed Jim her notebook and he read her neat script intently.

'Well Jenny, it looks like you knew what I needed before I did, as usual. You realise you are irreplaceable; I hope ShamOil will give you a decent pay increase this year. In the meantime as well as preparing my brilliant presentation, please make our Dublin travel arrangements.'

18

'Our?'

'Yes – **our** travel arrangements; something tells me you may have to step in at the last minute to take my place. An urgent appointment is likely to come up, promoting world peace will always take precedence over "helping businesses to grow sustainably and thereby creating employment opportunities and building successful communities".' Retorted Jim concluding with a gasp; thinking sentences ought not to be so long without punctuation.

Then he continued: 'At the very least you will have to be there to field any questions. There is no way I can ad lib answers to random credit questions. Please remember that while credit is a passion for you, it is just a front for me.' Only the President of ShamOil, Oleg (Oily) Solovyov, and Jenny knew this so her dedication to carrying Jim's responsibilities was essential for the maintenance of his cover.

'Handling questions is fine but I don't do public speaking, I'll freeze!'

'I froze the first time I tried so I empathise. The trick is to practice and to rehearse, particularly the first couple of sentences, oh and to breath – three deep breaths before standing up will relax you. When the presentation is ready, you can present it to me alone so I can give you some tips. After that practice a few times in front of a mirror and, when you feel more confident, you can present it to a small group of colleagues. That will be an opportunity to practice in a "safe" situation. If you can talk to one, two or three people at a cocktail party you can speak to any size of audience. One tactic that works is to pick one person in the middle of the audience to address and zone-out the rest at the start. Practice will help you believe in your ability.'

'Okay, I'm always willing to learn a new skill, especially in aid of creating world peace. Will what we have discussed be enough content for 45 minutes?'

'No, I need something more controversial. Could we attack the number crunching approach? All those ratios you keep going on about, all that linear extrapolation. Also those simplistic three variable models that the acolytes of accounting worship as portents of the future need to be de-bunked. Give me some ammunition and I might even be able to muster up some enthusiasm, nay passion!'

'Right on! The rating agencies (a plague on them) have raised the traditional approach to *high art* so the next stage of **your** presentation could cover a brief review of how useless their approach has proven to be time and again. I can then provide a transparency that points out that the focus of the traditional approach is on numbers and the past. Whereas numbers are manipulated and anyway frozen at a point of time – or not available - and the misguided belief that models or assumptions based on the past can be used to predict the future. That will provide an opportunity for you to introduce *the alternative approach....* dadaagh!!' Exclaimed Jenny with a fanfare and a failed attempt to emulate the musical announcement produced when a computer terminal fired-up; nevertheless she looked very pleased with herself.

'Oh, and what exactly is the alternative approach?'

'Well it's not exact at all; it's more art and less science, less maths. Credit assessment and management are all about *people* – individuals and groups - and *managing the future*, so math's does not help much.'

'Wait one! I may not be a credit geek but I do remember a few things about business from night school and Rapid Results College. I must be missing something though; we are talking about giving credit to companies that have balance sheets, income statements and cash flow statements, aren't we? So plenty of numbers to play with, ratios and Zeeeee scores and cash flow models, plenty of scope to have numbers provide **the** answer and exonerate us if something goes wrong. Traditional analysis and assessment worked so well for years, why change, why go all future conjecture and psychoanalytical on the credit profession?'

'Because there is nothing linear about the future anymore, sure after WWII each year in business was N% better so accountants could budget and managers could meet budget and customer-companies were stable with business models that hardly changed. However that has not been the case for decades, as Gary Hamel wrote in *Leading the Revolution*; 'change has changed, it is no longer additive, no longer does it move in a straight (predictable) line, change is discontinuous, abrupt, (and) seditious.' Oh and Ian Angell, writing in the *New Barbarian Manifesto* focussed our attention on the fact that the choices that we all make individually create the future. He put it this way; 'There can be no vision **of** the future, but there can and must be a vision **for** the future. A future that isn't there yet can't be discovered. It is created by men and women of vision, who are faced with the simple choice: **to create their own future**, or fall into somebody else's (and) be at the mercy of another's whim'.   I think I just formulated two more transparencies for you to talk to!' said Jenny with a broad smile that touched her brown-green eyes. She was obviously in her element, displaying the passion and delight of someone who thoroughly enjoyed her job.

'Well it's good to see you are enjoying yourself. Actually those ideas jive very well with many expressed by Ketan J Patel in his *The Master Strategist*, which I've just finished reading for the first time. Of course his closing remarks are more apposite the work of the Office of Peace than the world of credit. I'll read you an excerpt from pages 232 and 233, and then tell me if you agree: '...

"In this age of global access to people, places and the means to pay, there is nowhere to hide. We must find and deal better with those that fear and hate us or bear the consequences.

We will need to embrace a new language. This new language must come to change our minds. If we are successful, we will redefine **power** to mean the enhancement of freedoms; **purpose** will come to mean the pursuit of peace, prosperity and freedom, and **principle** will mean the pursuit of truth.

The resulting strategies will be more intuitive, more obtuse, more aspirational, more holistic, more technology-fused and, therefore, more uncomfortable.

Our success as humankind will only come if we put in place the institutions that will begin the work of demolishing the irrelevant, building the new and demolishing it once more when it becomes irrelevant.

We, therefore, stand at the door of an opportunity to seize the greatest personal power. We also stand at the door of the greatest opportunity in history – to **create an Age of Peace, Prosperity and Freedom**."

'Well that certainly is thought provoking but I will have to read it again before I'll be able to comment sensibly.'

'I understand; since I was reading the closing paragraphs you probably need to read the book before commenting. Here borrow my copy – my signed by the Author copy – and read it at your leisure.'

With that Jenny departed to attend to daily routine, chasing up invoices due to be paid the next week was top of her agenda. She always called buyers a week or so before due date in order to check that they had received the invoice, that they accepted the invoice as accurate and that they had made arrangements with their bank to pay the invoice on the due date. Jenny knew very well that most instances of overdue invoices are caused by either actual or claimed non-receipt of the invoice or a dispute relating to the accuracy of the invoice. She liked to 'eliminate' such excuses ahead of the due date to ensure that payment was always received on time.

Chapter 3

London 1990 January

Jim returned to the task of preparing for his planned meeting with F W de Klerk. He still had a lot of research to cover before he would be able to note the points he would wish to make. He lifted a pink folder marked "FOR YOUR EYES ONLY" from his drawer and laid it open on his desk. The first page – under the name and logo of the Office of Peace – bore the title:

Briefing Notes for Meeting with F W de Klerk
Prepared for Agent James E Cricket
Research Team - January 1990

While reading the report, Jim noted the following key points:

Ancestors arrived in the Cape in 1686.
Later generations were farmers (*boere* in Afrikaans) and took part in the Great Trek inland in order to escape British rule in the Eastern Cape. Some hoped to settle inland from Port Natal, others were determined to find a way across the Drakensberg Mountains and set up an independent state in the interior.
Three de Klerk family members died when Piet Retief's land grant negotiating delegation of about 68 souls was murdered on orders of the Zulu Chief Dingane in February 1838.
Subsequently the associated group of would-be settlers, about 470, including over 200 non-Zulu helpers and their families (+/- 180 children in total), were exterminated by Zulu impis at a place now called Weenen (*weeping* in Afrikaans) in what is now the province of Natal.
On December 16, 1838, the day still remembered by the Afrikaner nation every year as "The Day of the Vow" some 470 boere or voortrekkers overcame a Zulu force of over 10,000, inflicting more than 3,000 casualties. The battle has become known as The Battle of Blood River, because the river around which it took place ran red with blood on that day. (Note to self, lookup *impi*)

At this point Jim put down the file, swung round in his chair and gazed out of his second floor, corner office window. Wigmore Street, at its junction with James Street and Mandeville Place/Thayer Street was quiet. It was that time of day just before the lunch-time rush to the local eateries was due to commence. A few figures darted along the pavements, well protected in overcoats and hats against the bone biting wind that whipped around the corners of the buildings. Leaves and the occasional pieces of litter shifted or sailed on the wind from place to place. The sky was grey, heavy with cloud, which reflected Jim's mood. He had only begun his research but already wondered how he could possibly persuade FW to embrace his brother South Africans. The heavy burden of history that he and his fellow Afrikaner supporters had inherited would surely thwart Jim's efforts. What had been reported to have occurred in 1838 had been reinforced in their minds every year from childhood. Jim consoled himself with the thought that times change and people change and returned to reading the file, and jotting down notes.

A member of the National Party all his adult life – now 54 years old – considered to be a hard-line/conservative dedicated to enforcing the repressive principles institutionalised by former Presidents. One of whom, Hans Strijdom, was his uncle.
His grandfather was a founder member of the National Party in 1914; having been twice captured and imprisoned by the British during the Boer War.
FW was elected State President after a general election (only white citizens voted) in September 1989. His predecessor – PW Botha – resigned in August having stubbornly hung onto the Presidency despite having suffered a major stroke in January 1989.
Immediately President FW implemented changes – first woman member of the cabinet appointed – industrialists brought into the cabinet – removed restrictions on protest marches – ended segregation of beaches, parks, toilets and restaurants.
Released political prisoners, Govan Mbeki and the rest of the ANC leaders, except Nelson Mandela

'Ah', thought Jim, 'a glimmer of light, bold moves by FW; for a man living in his context, very bold moves. There is a spark of hope that he could move South Africa decisively forward along the road towards peace and reconciliation.'

24

Then, Lee Wei Ming broke the silence with a perfunctory knock at Jim's door. Wei Ming, the department's collateral management specialist, strode forward and then perched on the edge of the visitors' chair opposite Jim. He placed a sheet of printed paper on the desk and slid it forward for Jim's attention.

'Jim, zao shang hao! Nihao ma?'

'Hello Mr Lee, I'm fine. How about you? You look stressed,' said Jim as he closed and turned the FW file face down.

'Not so much stressed as annoyed. I've had to postpone lunch with Mike Rhodes, that's the third time. There's a crude cargo due to load at the Bonny Terminal, offshore Nigeria, in five days and the LC just arrived, opened by a bank which I don't know. I checked Bankers' Almanac and it doesn't even have a mention, it's the June, the latest edition of the Almanac so the bank must have been in existence for less than a year. It's for US$22 million.'

'Did the opening bank provide for confirmation? Oh, yes I see that now...."adding our confirmation",' said Jim, reading from the letter deposited on his desk by Wei Ming.

'Sure and the confirming bank is acceptable, but do you see the charge they will levy on us. Our trader is hopping mad 'cause his, correction our, margin is almost wiped out by the confirmation charges. To top that the confirming bank's central LC processing facility is in Leeds, so it took ten days for the LC to be turned around. It probably sat on some signatory's desk for a week. Now we have no time to sort out an alternative confirming bank.'

'Agreed we can't afford to delay the vessel loading and risk incurring demurrage charges, which would push the deal into the loss-making category. Of course our production affiliate will still make money but ShamOil Supply and Trading will be out of pocket! Wei Ming please ask someone in Treasury if we have any dealings with this confirming bank, if so call our Relationship Manager there and negotiate the confirmation fee. Unless otherwise instructed, banks direct LCs for confirmation to a panel of their relationship banks, by rotation, in order to provide lucrative side income for those banks. That enables the opening bank to negotiate better rates for their own transactional business handled by their relationship banks.

The upshot is that the LC beneficiary of such confirmations is charged the 'published' rate, like the 'rack rate' of a hotel room, in other words the highest rate. If the confirming bank has a relationship with us, a relationship overlooked in their Leeds processing office, they will have room to reduce the fee.'

'Good plan; I'll tackle that straight away. What are you working on now?' asked Wei Ming pointedly glancing at the file in front of Jim. 'You seemed to be very deep in thought when I interrupted you.'

'Oh, Jenny and I will be attending a GCMG conference in Dublin. I've just been doing some research for that trip, it made me think how important it is for us to add value. I'm regularly reminded by front office that we are a "cost centre". We need to change that perception; I don't want to work for a cost centre, that's totally a negative concept!'

'Anyway, why are we paying the confirmation fee on the LC?' asked Jim, deftly switching the subject back to business.

'Our trader agreed to do that, he says it was a potential "deal breaker". You know that some buyers don't understand the concept of "bank risk"; even some of our competitors accept low rated banks without confirmation.'

'Well in that case he or his operations person could have given us plenty of warning. You could have minimised the cost by negotiating with several potential confirming banks and nominating our choice.

Please chat with the head of operations and draft an agreed process so we avoid this issue in future. Let's finalise that when I return from Dublin.'

'Okay, boss', with that Wei Ming left Jim to return to his research. Jim immediately locked away his file, picked up his tourist guide to Dublin and headed out the door, destined for his favourite café in James Street.

Jim was pleased to read the description of the conference venue hotel:

A national treasure built in 1824. The Shelbourne Hotel has been magnificently restored while keeping its historic charm. The Shelbourne is a luxury hotel in Dublin city centre overlooking St. Stephen's Green, Europe's grandest garden square. Ideally situated close to Dublin's cultural and historic buildings, The Shelbourne offers a great location from where you can visit the majestic St. Patrick's Cathedral and Trinity College. Explore shops on Grafton Street or visit the Guinness Storehouse.

The mention of Grafton Street particularly piqued his interest, a good place to soak in some local atmosphere, albeit probably designed for tourists.

Chapter 4

Dublin 1990 January

On January 28, 1990 Jim landed in Dublin and checked into The Shelbourne for what he hoped would be a fateful first visit to the Emerald Isle. A place steeped in history, most of the recorded bits involving violence and depravation. However a place populated by the most charming people, most of whom displayed a sharp sense of humour and spoke with a lilting accent that required concentration of the foreign visitor.

Jim had arranged an early flight so that he would have time after lunch to explore the area surrounding the hotel. He was particularly keen to see St. Stephen's Green before sunset.

St. Stephen's Green was not at its best at the time of year, the trees were bare of leaves and the fine light rain that fell that afternoon kept all but the hardy visitor away from the park. Weather that Jim learned the local inhabitants refer to as 'soft', much to his quiet amusement. Nevertheless he enjoyed the invigorating walk and could judge from the layout of the formal beds and pathways that the Green would be a very attractive setting in spring and summer. Jim briefly admired the grand gateway that stood at the corner of the Green, opposite the end, or beginning of Grafton Street.

Passing a pub in Grafton Street, Jim noticed a poet busker sheltering from the rain close to the doorway. The youth had a board propped against the wall announcing a list of poems he would recite on request, for a small fee. His list included the offer to recite one of his own poems for an even smaller fee. Jim chose the latter; he was fascinated, having seen many street entertainers in cities from Moscow to Vienna, to London but never before a poet busker. The poet's poem was a reference to the Warsaw Pact intervention in Czechoslovakia in 1968, when tanks rolled into Prague to squash the nascent reforms being introduced by then Prime Minister Dubcek. Unfortunately, although the poem consisted of only four or five lines, Jim could only recall the title;

"For Dubcek I die"

When he returned to his hotel room, Jim found a blinking red button on his phone indicating he had one or more voice messages. The first was from Jenny, announcing in a very excited voice that she had arrived and found her room 'amazing', and she would meet him at the pre-conference cocktail party at 7pm. The second was from his contact on FW de Klerk's staff. The SA President could see him at 9:30 sharp next morning. Jim was to report to the Princess Grace Suite on the second floor of The Shelbourne at 9:20 sharp! 'Well that solves one mystery' thought Jim. He had wondered where they would meet since South Africa did not have diplomatic relations with the Republic of Eire, hence there was no SA Embassy to provide a venue.

Jim next checked the conference agenda and a broad grin spread across his face. He was due to present his paper to the conference at 9am.

Jim was able to watch Jenny launch their presentation from the back of the room, before he flashed a 'thumbs up' and slipped out to keep his very important appointment. In fact Jenny had made an excellent start, despite her expressions of anxiety and nerves. Obviously the practice had paid off, and once she was past the initial remarks her passion for the subject took over.

When he stepped out of the conference hall Jim's mind was filled with his immediate task, a task the achievement of which seemed only a remote possibility. As he took the stairs he revised the points he had jotted down, the points he planned to make to FW. He fervently hoped they would make a positive difference:

- Only a negotiated understanding among the leaders of the whole population will ensure lasting peace.
- Alternative is growing violence, tension and conflict. That is unacceptable and in nobody's interest.
- Drastic change requires a totally new and just constitutional dispensation
- Put petty politics aside and focus on discussing the future, a future characterised by peace, prosperity and freedom

A burley man in a suit, his blond hair shorn in a 'crew cut' style checked Jim's identity, his invitation, and 'patted him down' to ensure he was unarmed, before ushering him into the suite.

On entering what was the lounge, Jim was a little shaken when he noticed the man seated in the corner, to his left, was virtually the twin of the one who had just checked him at the door. However his attention immediately shifted to the silhouette of the man seated at a desk, facing the window. 'Good morning Mr President', Jim ventured, as he advanced a couple of paces into the room 'I'm James Cricket, it's so very good of you to agree to meet with me.'

Without turning the man at the desk replied, 'Ahh Meneer Cricket, ja rright on time, welkom, welkom!'

At this Jim was shocked because the voice and accent, certainly did not match those of FW de Klerk. He had heard the President speak English on taped interviews and speeches, of course with an Afrikaans accent but certainly not as strong.

The silhouette rose and turned, with a little difficulty given the background light from the window Jim made out a man who looked like FW and carried himself like FW, but clearly was not the President! He was dressed for the part though, a tailored dark blue lounge suit, white dress shirt, starched, with double cuffs, gold cuff-links – with some sort of crest emblem difficult to make out at a distance - and a blue tie. Not plain blue, a Springbok Centenary tie. Jim took a step back as the man advanced. Was this some kind of trap set up by the forces against peace? The security guard seated in the corner didn't move. As the FW look-alike advanced he smiled and thrust out his right hand, announcing, 'I'm Danie, Danie van der Merwe veerrry pleased to meet you Jim or do you prefer Jiminy?' With that he roared with laughter!

Jim proffered his hand instinctively, his brain still in a buzz as he tried to fathom what was happening. Danie fixed him with an iron grip squeezing Jim's signet ring into the adjoining fingers, the pain helped Jim re-focus. He resisted Danie's attempt to dominate by holding his hand in the vertical as Danie tried to turn his hand on top.

'Sorry man, about the disappointment, you won't be meeting President de Klerk today!' Danie continued. Then indicating an arm-chair, 'Sit, sit, take the weight off your feet man. I'll explain everrrything. You see, old FW has upset both sides of the house lately so I'm his double, here to confuse anyone out there with 'ideas'. FW told me to give you hees sincere apology and to thank you for helping make his Dublin 'visit' look more genuine. We know you will keep our little secret.'

'Well I appreciate your President's expression of confidence in my discretion, but isn't he supposed to meet with the Irish President later today? How will you keep that quiet?'

'Oh Pres. Paddy Hillery is a good sport, fully on-board, I don't know why – perhaps hee iss ah rrugby fan. Only Paddy and hees security mensa know to expect a double. Anyway we are happy for anyone with 'ideas' to know about this visit, just keeping it from the media.'

Danie's propensity to mix Afrikaans words into his sentences was a little confusing but Jim managed to understand the sense. 'So where is President de Klerk - the genuine article that is?'

'Aagh man, last I heard he was at hees holiday home at Hermanus in the Cape, probably walking the beach and talking to the seagulls, relaxing. He has a big speech to give on Vrydag, you know!'

'Hmm yes, I assume you will not be doing any sight-seeing during this visit,' continued Jim, struggling to keep some sort of conversation alive.

'Haha, yes, I'm here to be seen at a distance only. Well I would liike to chat longer but must not be late for the President's appointment with the President!' Danie replied, mercifully putting an end to Jim's discomfort.

Then, after another bone crushing handshake and an exchange of farewell pleasantries, Jim found himself out in the corridor. He was immediately struck by a depressing sense of disappointment. All the research, all the rehearsing and thinking through the meeting with FW, then nothing. Well less than nothing actually - a bizarre meeting with a very affable doppelgänger. At this point he could not face going back to the conference directly.

Ten minutes later Jim was seated in a corner of the hotel bar lounge nursing a double espresso, staring out across the mid-morning, quite road at the winter scene. After a while he gave himself a pep-talk (FW would just have to manage without his advice), pulled himself together and re-focused on the GCMG conference.

Jenny's presentation was a triumph. Many questions and her confident answers generated much discussion amongst the audience, causing her to over-run her time allocation. However no one complained about the curtailed coffee break, in fact delegates continued discussing the points raised in small groups as they 'net-worked'. The conference organiser was thrilled with the outcome and immediately asked Jenny to be a panel member for the open forum portion at the next conference.

Jim had not been missed at all but he found solace in Jenny's success. He had provided Jenny with the opportunity and encouragement she needed to master public speaking. Her achievement reflected positively on Jim and his leadership style, so his Dublin trip was not a complete loss after all.

Chapter 5

London 1990 February

After a couple of days spent clearing work backlog in the office, Jim asked Jenny and Wei Ming to join him for a team meeting on Friday afternoon.

On Friday, February 2nd, Jim pushed to the back of his mind thoughts of FW de Klerk's speech due at 2pm London time. The media seemed confident FW would announce nothing new in his opening address to Parliament in Cape Town; with the exception of the much anticipated release of Nelson Mandela and perhaps more oppressive regulations, so there was no need to follow the speech.

He deliberately arranged a long lunch with his friend and former colleague Roger (French pronunciation) Dreyfus. He reserved a table at Odin's, their favourite restaurant situated on Devonshire Street, a short walk from his office. The restaurant had a luxurious ambiance, with comfortable furnishings and a fine art collection that covered almost every square centimetre of the walls. Both amateur art and wine buffs, Jim and Roger found this 'bolt-hole' a perfect place to reminisce or debate, and to solve humanity's problems over a glass (a well provisioned glass) of Châteauneuf-du-Pape and an excellent repast.

Roger was Head of Trade Finance Operations with a major French trade bank and a world renowned expert on Letters of Credit. They had shared a room in a Hall of Residence at Exeter University and later worked together in the foreign department of a bank.

After almost two hours passed very pleasantly they parted outside; as Roger hailed a black cab and headed back to his office, Jim sauntered down Marylebone High Street, his mind still going over some of their conversation. He was jerked back into present reality when a fire engine engaged its siren as it turned into the street behind him and started to wend its way through the traffic towards Wigmore Street.

Jim had planned a 'busy' afternoon of routine, beginning with the team meeting at 3pm. Top of the agenda was a review of the GCMG Dublin conference and what lessons had been learnt.

Jenny came to the meeting armed with copies of her presentation transparencies and some of the other presentations. Jim congratulated her again on the success of her presentation and Wei Ming interrogated her on several points, which she enthusiastically explained. Jenny then progressively introduced two other key presentations, which she thought warranted consideration and discussion. The one related to single-name credit risk insurance absorbed their attention for almost 30 minutes.

Suddenly their concentration was shattered as Jim's office door burst open! In strode Simon Jones breathless with excitement, his athletic frame almost filled the doorway, as he advanced without apology for his rude intrusion. Simon was the Head of Crude Oil Trading (Eastern Hemisphere), although obviously with Welsh heritage, given his family name, he was born in England, he had even played rugby for England some 14 years ago. At 36 he still 'worked out' regularly as evidenced by his general healthy appearance.

Simon was already speaking and opening a copy of The Independent, late edition, as he advanced; 'He has uuh, it's amazing, historic, de Klerk has surprised the world! Here listen to this, "de Klerk has announced his government is committed to a full democracy, with majority rule in a unitary state, committed to equal justice for all under a human rights manifesto, no discrimination, and a free economy." The entire edifice of apartheid has been dismantled in a half hour speech!'

'Allister Sparks, the editor, is quoted as saying, "My God, he's done it all." Bishop Tutu apparently giggled when he said, "Just wait till de Klerk sits down with Tambo. They will discover how South African they both are!"

'President de Klerk's concluding remarks included an invitation to the ANC; he said "Walk through the open door and take your place at the negotiating table."'

34

'What?   That is unbelievable!' Jim responded, astonished. 'What about Mandela, was he mentioned at all?'

'Only once, near the end of the speech. He will be released in a few days, with no preconditions!'

Wei Ming, a little puzzled at this point, chipped in 'Simon this is of course good news, but why are you so excited? You don't have any SA or political connections, do you?'

'Rugby of course', Jenny re-joined. 'The Springboks missed the first World Cup in '87 because of the sports boycott.'

'Correctamundo Jenny! Only a matter of time before my club team can tour SA again....' Simon's sentence trailed off as he turned on heel and left the office as abruptly as he had arrived.

After a few moments of silence Jim ventured, 'Well our meeting seems a little lame after all that excitement; let's adjourn to James Street for coffee. I'll try once more to explain the game of cricket to you Wei Ming.   South Africa can field a pretty strong team. Fetch your coats and I'll meet you at the stairs.' As soon as Jenny had left the office Jim placed his copy of her presentation in File 13, also known as his paper recycle bin, picked up his coat and followed suit.

Chapter 6

London 1990 February

On February 11, 1990 Nelson Mandela was released from prison. Jim was in euphoric mood as he returned to his office around 3pm on Monday, after a rather long celebratory lunch. Having watched the historic event that was beamed live to pretty much every television screen in the world the previous day, he had felt compelled to celebrate.

His phone was ringing when he came through the doorway, so without removing his coat he reached across the desk to lift the receiver. 'Good afternoon, Jim Cricket!'

Oily Solovyov was on the line, 'Hey Jimbo, how's the peace business going?'

'Hello Oily, so good to hear from you, peace business is going well. You know Mandela was released yesterday?'

'Yes! Not much oil in SA though, plenty of gold, diamonds, platinum, even copper, lots of coal and some gas off-shore Mossel Bay, but no oil. However there's lots of oil in the Soviet Union.'

'Yes, but that is pretty much out of bounds for US companies, isn't it?'

'That's what I want to talk to you about Jim. You know Gorbachev's **perestroika,** meaning 'restructuring', and **glasnost**, meaning 'openness', policies are really gaining momentum, but too many Soviets find the radical changes hard to accept. With the right kind of encouragement and help the Soviet Union could break up, the Warsaw Pact wither away and the Cold War come to an end. Great opportunities to improve the future prospects of millions of global citizens beckon, if we can avoid sliding back into the old ways. This is where you come into the picture Jim, well I mean the Office of Peace of course.'

'What exactly do you have in mind Oily?'

'ShamOil participating in oil production and export in the Soviet Union of course! I've floated an idea with the OoP for you to undertake some sort of mission to support Gorbachev. They are 'thinking about it' so, while we are waiting I would like you to prepare, you know, research the people, the history, read War and Peace, learn the language, that sort of thing.'

'I can do that Oily, well everything except learn the language while we wait. Learning the language would take years! It's well known that Russian is one of the most complex and expressive languages in the world. You are fluent, aren't you?'

'Yes, thanks to my dear Mother's persistence. I don't mean for you to become fluent, just learn the basics; greetings, reading the Cyrillic alphabet, that sort of thing. In fact I have already asked Simon to have Russian language lessons arranged for London staff, on a voluntary basis of course. He has suggested two hours twice a week over the 'lunch' period. If things turn out well ShamOil will definitely be involved in the Soviet Union so we need employees to learn Russian. I trust you will be one of the first to volunteer for lessons.'

'Yes, of course, that's very generous of you Oily', said Jim immediately regretting his phrasing in case it was interpreted as sarcastic. Fortunately Oily took his words as genuine and their conversation ended as amicably as it had begun.

At about 6:30pm Jim headed home, leaving the office he set-off in the direction of Bond Street Underground Station as was his usual habit. On the way though he stopped at the book shop in St Christopher's Place and bought a reference book, *The Soviet Union* by Lidiya Dubinskaya (Author) and James Riordan (Translator). It was rather bulky publication but hopefully a good place to begin his research.

At home, after dinner, Jim took the fake-leather bound two volumes of War and Peace from the bookshelf they had adorned for more than15 years. After dusting them off he opened volume one, and recalled his first brief encounter with the book when it arrived from Readers' Digest, neatly packed in a brown cardboard Royal Mail box. Yes, he remembered the preface by the translator offering his abject apology for being unable to do full justice to the beauty and power of the original Russian text.

Then he came across the 'caste list', a vital part of the book for any reader who dared to venture further. Jim however had not ventured further, having struggled to read through the list of characters he had placed the book on the shelf where it had impressed guests ever since. Now though he would have to make the effort to read the tome. Perhaps the Russian language lessons would help him wrap his tongue around the character names, so he could comfortably proceed. Deftly replacing the volumes back in their accustomed position, Jim resolved to return to the Tolstoy classic when his Russian studies had progressed sufficiently.

Tuesday brought another crisis for Wei Ming.

'Boss, we have a problem!'

'What no 'Ni hao ma?' Not even a 'Ni hao'?'

'Oh, I'm sorry; I'm just a bit stressed. Hello, hello! Our crude trader is saying his deal with SimpleTrade is in trouble, they are insisting that we issue them a Documentary LC to cover the cargo that is supposed to load next week, he says it's a potential deal-breaker.'

'Jean-Francois knows that ShamOil only issues LCs to National Oil companies, like Egyptian General Petroleum Co and Nigerian National Petroleum Corp, only those companies that have to obtain LCs according to their local law. Ask him to provide you with SimpleTrade's credit or finance contact so you can explain how Payment Undertakings work. Where is SimpleTrade based?'

'They are based in Geneva. I have the contact details. SimpleTrade is run by two traders that used to work for Prasem; they recently started on their own. They claim to have a rich backer and of course have plenty of good contacts. They have to open an LC in favour of the crude supplier, but their bank will only do that on a back-to-back basis.'

'I understand - that is quite usual; which bank are they using? Presumably a major Swiss trade bank, is it Paribas, United Overseas Bank, Swiss Bank Corporation, Banque Nationale de Paris, or Société Générale?'

'United Overseas Bank, and before you ask, I checked; it is the Swiss UOB not the entirely different Singapore bank of the same name.'

'Good UOB know us so there will be no problem relating to authentication of our Payment Undertaking, and no need for us to have a bank countersignature appended. Here, Jenny wrote up the Payment Undertaking process a couple of months ago for another new supplier; please fax it to SimpleTrade, ask contracts to amend the contract to cover our obligation to issue the PU, and call UOB to alert them. Here are the details of my contact at UOB', said Jim as he wrote a note and then handed it to Wei Ming.

'By the way Jim, since we produce lots of crude oil every day, why do we have to buy crude?'

'Unfortunately a lot of the crude we produce is not ideal input for our refineries. Our refinery managers require crude with certain specifications so they can produce the best possible yield from a value point of view. That is to say the highest proportion of high value product such as jet and the least of low value fuel oil, based on the capabilities of the refinery. That's why we sell a lot of the crude we produce and buy a lot of the crude we refine. It seems crazy but makes sense. Older refineries are less able to deal with the so-called heavy crudes that we have to tap more and more, because 'light' crude reserves are being depleted.'

'Hmm, so crude is not all the same. Okay, thanks. I'll tackle SimpleTrade now!' With that Wei Ming left the office.

Jim turned his attention back to early preparation for his next assignment. He had found *The Soviet Union* rather heavy going, as well as being heavy to carry on his daily commute, so had searched for an alternative. Fortunately he had chanced across what was turning out to be an excellent and relatively light book covering negotiating Soviet style aptly called,

Negotiating with the Soviets by Raymond F. Smith. Jim had been particularly attracted by the review on the back cover that, in part, stated:

"He (the Author) explains the persistent Soviet preoccupation with the 'context' of negotiations and the respective 'hierarchy' of the partners. The findings are less original than the author's interpretation of the Soviet approach as a synthesis of political culture, ideology, and dialectical reasoning. Soviet continuity of style remains despite Gorbachev's penchant for 'initiative' and ability to 'compromise'. Because of Smith's commitment to promoting 'understanding and effectiveness' in U.S.-Soviet exchange rather than notions of 'right or wrong', his prescription for more 'bipartisan' American foreign policy is especially convincing." *Zachary T. Irwin, Behrend Coll., Pennsylvania State Univ., Erie. Copyright 1989 Reed Business Information, Inc.*

Although Jim would freely admit that he struggled to understand the concept of 'dialectical reasoning' he was gleaning potentially invaluable insight into the Russian psyche, especially their concept of truth. Jim realised that this would be particularly important in respect of contracts. It was made clear that Russians view contracts as statements of the agreed true position of the parties at a point in time. As long as the context within which a contract is agreed does not change significantly they will honour the contract terms. However if the context changes, then the 'truth' of the circumstances has changed so it becomes legitimate to expect one's counterparty to renegotiate the contract for mutual benefit, within the new context.

Jim wondered how such an approach would sit with the US Legal Counsel for ShamOil; he suspected it would not be welcome. After-all 'a contract is a contract', is the Western approach – no compromise, no renegotiation, simply go away and perform as promised!

Jim turned to the fax Wei Ming had dropped on his desk in the meantime. Oil production, trading, refining and distribution is a 24/365 business after all. Time is always 'of the essence'.

....

Wei Ming's Fax to SimpleTrade:

ShamOil Supply & Trading UK Ltd
Wigmore Street
London
United Kingdom
1990.02.13

FAX

SimpleTrade Associates SA
Geneva
Switzerland

Dear Sirs;

Reference Purchase/Sale Contract # SO-ST001-123456 Dated 1990.02.09

Please note that, as verbally agreed between our Mr J-F Piton and your M le Branché today, the above referenced contract will be amended by the addition or substitution of the following clauses:

"Credit: At least five days prior to delivery Buyer will send to Seller's bank with a copy to Seller's financial contact a Purchase Confirmation/Payment Undertaking in a format acceptable to Seller (bank and text will be provided)."

and

"Assignment: This agreement will not be assignable by either party without the written consent of the other, which shall not be unreasonably withheld. However, in the event payment is not made by the Buyer on due date, Seller has the right to assign the financial rights under this agreement to a bank without the prior consent of the Buyer."

You will receive a formal contract amendment from our Contracts Team later today.

41

An explanatory note regarding the Payment Undertaking process is included with this fax.

Yours faithfully

Lee, Wei Ming   J E Cricket
Collateral Manager   Credit Manager
                                        Europe   Middle   East
                              Africa

....

After signing the cover letter Jim placed his copy, which included the explanatory note, in File 13 and returned the original to Wei Ming for despatch.

Chapter 7

London 1990 February

Jim's phone was ringing insistently as he walked into his office Wednesday morning, 'Hello, James Cricket!'

'Hello Jim! Willy Slater here, Office of Peace, how the devil are you?'

'Will, greetings! You really should switch to calling yourself Will or Bill. I'm fine, very pleased to see the progress being made in South Africa. Where are you?'

'Ottawa, Canada.'

'It must be just after four in the morning, why aren't you home in bed in Boston?'

'I've been shadowing the Open Skies Ministerial Conference since Sunday. It involved all NATO and Warsaw Pact Foreign Ministers. While you were enjoying live coverage from Cape Town, I was freezing; the city is under a blanket of snow.'

'Open Skies – why was that of interest to the OoP?'

'It was not, until we received word that Baker and Genscher planned to hatch a plot to initiate negotiation of a treaty to finally re-unite Germany. Genscher – I assume you know he is the West German Foreign Minister - well he had correctly, as it turns out, sensed that the Soviets have no strategy in this respect. Anyway they managed to persuade Shevardnadze - after Shev' made several calls to Moscow - to agree to begin negotiations with the two parts of Germany and the four Occupying Powers. The Soviets probably think negotiations will drag on for years, but we discovered that Genscher aims for reunification by this Fall.'

'Wow that would be a major step forward for world peace. A peaceful, unified Germany with full sovereignty restored, after 45 years of divided occupation. What are they calling the negotiations the two-by-four? Haha, 2x4, sounds like a piece of lumber, hehe!' Jim giggled.

'Well no, the negotiating group is being called the 'Two-Plus-Four Ministerial Meeting', all parties have equal status. On a serious note James, the negotiations have a lot of ground to cover, many thorny issues, so the Coordinator would like you to be as close to the progress as possible over the coming months. It will be imperative to be in a position to help overcome any stumbling blocks that may arise.'

'Thank you William, it will be my pleasure to do whatever I can to help.'

'Good, I will send you a briefing paper soon after I return to Boston. Now I must sleep. Let's talk again soon, ciao!'

'Goodbye Will, sleep well!' Jim, now deep in thought, replaced the receiver, hung up his overcoat and stood staring out his office window. The past few months had produced significant and totally unexpected steps forward on the road to peace. Who, after learning of the tragedy that occurred in Beijing in June 1989, would have thought such momentous changes could occur peacefully. The possibility that more progress was within the grasp of world leaders, however tenuous, was exciting. The hopeful feeling took Jim's mind back 22 years to the glorious summer of 1968.

On August 16, 1968, during the summer break, after his first year reading Business Economics at Exeter, Jim arrived in Prague. He was accompanied by his room-mate Roger (French pronunciation) Dreyfus. They had been invited to spend two weeks as guests of Jim's uncle Gerald, his mother's brother, a Foreign Office employee.

Gerald had been educated at Harrow and Sandhurst. After graduating from the Royal Military College, eighth out of his class of 150, he was commissioned a Second Lieutenant in the 4th Queen's Own Hussars in 1957. After five years, having attained the position of Adjutant, with the rank of Captain, in the Queen's Royal Irish Hussars - with which his regiment was amalgamated in 1958 – he left the army and joined the Foreign Office.

The excitement engendered by the changes and hope embodied in the epithet 'Prague Spring' was palpable as they stepped off the plane at Ruzyne International Airport.

Large as life, Gerald stood at the foot of the aircraft steps to greet his nephew. Jim was surprised to see Gerald on the tarmac, airside. Perhaps the family rumour that he was actually MI6 was true, thought Jim, as he matched Gerald's broad grin and met his piecing blue eyes set beneath tussled, thick, light-brown hair. A firm hand shake followed, and then Gerald took charge. 'So you must be Roger Dreyfus, welcome, welcome!' he effused.

'Good morning sir' Roger replied, as they shook hands warmly.

'No, no 'sir', call me 'Gerald' please, I had enough of 'sir' in the army. Okay, let's gather your luggage, head home and get you settled.'

As Gerald talked they made their way into the terminal building, breezed through Immigration, picked up their bags and jumped into the Embassy car. Jim noticed that Gerald was on first name terms with security and immigration officers, variously exchanging banter and warm greetings, asking about their family members and commenting on the latest football match. Most of the time he spoke in English, but confidently used Czech when necessary.

Roger was understandably nervous on arriving, his parents had moved to England only shortly before the Nazi occupation of France. Tragically the rest of his extended family subsequently perished in the concentration camps. Although he was born after the war ended the transmitted memories and emotions of his parents and older brother weighed heavily on his mind.

Jim had briefed Gerald who was obviously determined to make Roger feel at ease, part of the family. When they were seated in the Embassy car Gerald outlined some of the arrangements he had made for their visit. 'Roger, as Jim may have explained I tutor an English class at the Institute of Culture and Journalism, part of the Charles University in Prague. I'm going to be busy so a couple of my language students have volunteered to host you; they are keen to show you some of the culture, sport, and student activities. They will no doubt introduce you to some of their friends. They are eager to practice their English skills and learn about student life on the other side of the 'iron curtain'.

'Thank you sir, ah Gerald, it is very kind of you to make the arrangement. Please tell us their names so we can memorise them and not to be embarrassed, I have difficulty remembering some foreign names.'

'Certainly the man is called Beda, Beda Dudik, and the woman Irena, Irena Nesvadbová. So Beda and Irena not too difficult; Beda is Czech and Irena is Slovak. They are good friends from what I can discern and have a good sense of fun.'

At that point they reached the door of Gerald's apartment block, thanked the Embassy driver and made their way up two rather steep flights of stairs to his flat. The flat consisted of large rooms with high ceilings, it was spacious and light streamed in large windows in each room. Situated on the 'left bank' immediately to the North of Charles Bridge; 'Karluv Most' in Czech as Jim was determined to refer to the historic river crossing.

Jim and Roger were introduced to Gerald's housekeeper, a young woman from Hungary by the name of Kinia Gabor. Kinia had a lovely smile that lit up her eyes, although it revealed slightly crooked teeth, the legacy of poor dental care during childhood, Jim surmised.

Having been shown the room they were to occupy, with its outlook on the rear courtyard and the buildings that 'climbed' up the hill to the Castle district, the bathroom and kitchen, they repaired to the living room. Here they savoured a light lunch of sandwiches, cake and tea, which Kinia produced. While eating they enjoyed the glorious view of the Old Town across the broad, fast-flowing Vltava, and listened intently to a local news update from Gerald.

At the end of March, Alexander Dubcek had taken over as First Secretary of the Central Committee of the Communist Party and a new government was installed. Faced with a serious housing shortage, a failing economy and a chaotic transportation system the government immediately started implementing reforms. The reforms were approved by Dubcek, who had promised to abolish censorship, restrict the role of the secret police and introduce greater parliamentary rights when appointed. An article, *Two Thousand Words*, by Ludvik Vaculik, calling on the people to struggle against everything they considered bad, had emboldened many citizens, particularly intellectuals and artists. However hardliners within Czechoslovakia and throughout the Soviet bloc openly criticised the 'radical' reforms being introduced, together with the symbols of Western culture, such as jazz music, rock clubs, pop culture and mini-skirts.

'You will find for yourselves that there is a general feeling of euphoria on the streets and in the local media, but we are hearing that Dubcek has many enemies. Apparently he has felt obliged to reassure the Russians and other Soviet bloc leaders that Czechoslovakia remains loyal to Soviet Communist ideals and will not leave the Warsaw Pact.

Nevertheless when Warsaw Pact military manoeuvres in Czechoslovakia ended as planned last month, the troops didn't leave immediately. When they did leave they only moved to positions across the border where they remain, hovering like an ominous, dark storm cloud. We are all very aware of what happened in Hungary in 1956.'

'Oh, I'm not.' Jim interrupted, 'Sorry my knowledge of History is lacking.'

'The Soviets rolled tanks into Budapest. After a violent revolution, the Hungarian people established a government with a self-determination agenda. It started talking about withdrawal from the Warsaw Pact and declared neutrality. The Soviet Politburo initially withdrew troops from Budapest and a brief period of calm ensued. Unfortunately the declaration of neutrality handed hard-liners in the Soviet Politburo the means with which to reverse the decision to pull back its forces. A shameful bloodbath took place, and any resistance was crushed. The then Prime Minister was arrested and later executed, and the country was purged of reformists and so called radical intellectuals.'

'Well, I can understand why people here will be worried about history repeating itself', Roger ventured.

'Yes, indeed!' said Gerald as he rose from his chair, picked up his briefcase and started towards the door. 'I have work to do so I must hike up the hill to the Embassy tout de suite. On her way home, Kinia will show you a good local restaurant, where you will find a repast adequate to your needs this evening. I will be in late tonight so will probably next see you at breakfast, at around 9:30. Sleep well!'

Chapter 8

Prague 1968 August

Jim woke to the sound of Roger's alarm clock – Roger was the organised one of the two. They had enjoyed a relaxing evening, with good food washed down with a glass of eminently acceptable local beer, accompanied by live music from a resident quartet. Well rested and in good spirits they were greeted by a smiling Kinia and the aromas of breakfast, as they entered the dining room. The sun streamed in the windows at a rather acute angle at that time so blinds were drawn down, obscuring the view.

Gerald was already at the table, looking as if he had only just arrived home, dressed as he had been when he had left the house after lunch. Nevertheless he greeted them cheerfully, without a hint of exhaustion, and bid them 'tuck in' to the morning meal.

'Well good to hear you enjoyed the evening. As you no doubt guessed I have been busy, report writing can keep one up all night.' He added with a wry smile that indicated there was somewhat more to his activities than paper-work.

'Saturday is my sleep catch-up day gentlemen, so I've arranged for Beda and Irena to arrive here at about eleven. They will be introducing you to the delights of Prague; they are a charming pair so I'm sure you will be hosted in fine style and meet a lot of interesting people. No doubt you will end up at the Reduta Jazz Club, but if they don't suggest it be sure to make a request. It is not to be missed for atmosphere and fine music.'

'Dinner tomorrow, here at 7pm sharp, we can catch-up then. Sunday is Kinia's day of rest, but I will be working I'm afraid. Anyway you should know your way around the transport system, such as it is, by then so you have a free day. Do nothing or go exploring.' With that Gerald excused himself from the table and left the room in search of some well-earned rest.

Beda and Irena were well known to Kinia, who welcomed them when they arrived shortly after eleven, as expected. After the four introduced themselves they set off on foot to explore the Castle District. They took a light lunch at a café on Mostecká, where their hosts introduced them to some fellow students and they spent a couple of hours chatting. Politics and sport were the main topics, although Jim and Roger were thoroughly quizzed regarding fashion, music and technology trends in England. Everyone seemed to speak quite freely, contrary to Jim's expectations. He found this refreshing, however he did feel obliged to point out from time to time that not all was perfect at home, since democratic capitalist societies faced a number of challenges.

Leaving the café the four strolled across Charles Bridge, admiring and discussing the stunning scenery en route to the Old Town Square. There they watched the Astronomical Clock 'perform' on the hour and agreed that it was much more than a mere clock. Roger bought a postcard featuring the ancient masterpiece, intending to write home at the next opportunity. They rested again under the shade of an awning stretched out across the front of a restaurant, sampling more local beer, snacking on pretzels, and listening to a Gypsy trio playing traditional tunes. People watching and conversation with friends seemed to Jim to be universal relaxation pursuits.

The group fell silent around 4:20. Jim checked his watch when he realised they were silent and recalled, 'Ah Angels must be passing overhead.'

'What do you mean?' Beda queried.

'Oh it's something my mother believes. When a group falls silent the time is usually 20 minutes past or 20 minutes to the hour, and when that is the case the silence has occurred because "Angels are passing overhead". Of course there is no way to prove or disprove that statement, but it is strange how often a group silence occurs at those times.'

With that Irena shook off the day-dream she was enjoying. 'We are going our separate ways from here gentlemen, but we will fetch you from Gerald's place at 9 tonight. The Reduta is our destination this evening. I hope you like jazz music. Well, if not, you will after tonight. There's a tenor sax player in the visiting band, who my friends are raving about. Dutch, they say he is a rebel, 28 but still loves to be different; he has caused controversy in Amsterdam where he manages a jazz club. It's their last night in Prague, so we expect a storming performance.'

'Before we part, is there anything you specially want to see?' asked Beda.

'Yes, there is, if it's convenient' Roger ventured. 'The Old-New Synagogue, do you know of it?'

'I certainly do, it's the oldest still existing synagogue in Europe, it has been in use for over 700 years. It stands not far from here; you could pass it on your way back to Gerald's.'

'Here I'll draw you a map, so you don't waste time wondering about,' said Irena borrowing a pen from a passing waiter and reaching for a paper napkin.

'Will I have to wait outside, Roger? I don't have suitable headgear in my pocket like you,' ventured Jim.

'Any hat is acceptable, even your red tartan bunnet!'

'Red; I'll have you know it's the Stewart Royal Tartan.'

'But you are not a Scot! How can you justify wearing a tartan let alone a Royal Tartan?'

'As a loyal subject of Her Majesty, I'm entitled to wear this tartan!' Jim proclaimed.

'Well, with your sun burnt red face and your bunnet, standing there you look like a matchstick.' Irena chuckled. With that Roger burst into uncontrollable laughter, quickly joined by Beda.

Gasping to catch his breath, Roger spluttered, 'Irena you are so observant! Don't worry Jim, synagogues always have yarmulkes available for gentile visitors to cover their heads.' With that the friends parted.

After spending a fascinating hour or so taking in the solemn atmosphere, historic significance and interesting architecture of the Old-New Synagogue, Roger and Jim made their way along the cobbled streets. There was no need to hurry and plenty to see as they strolled back to Gerald's flat. The day had been full of interest and the night promised to be equally rewarding.

At 9 pm, true to their word, Irena and Beda arrived at Gerald's door. 'Reduta is in Národni Street, three blocks from Wenceslas Square. We have to take a bus then a tram. It's a small venue so we want to arrive before the jazz is supposed to begin at 9:30. I say "supposed to begin" because musicians seem to have a flexible sense of time,' Irena explained with a smile.

The tram was filled mainly with couples and small groups of friends, all seemed to be students. At the Národni Trida stop, in Spálená Street most occupants left the tram and they all wondered together along the otherwise quiet street, chatting amongst themselves. The atmosphere was relaxed and good natured banter could be heard exchanged as they made their way to Reduta. It seemed the tram had been filled with jazz fans.

At the corner with Národni they turned left and came across the entrance to Reduta almost immediately. The club was in the basement accessed down a flight of stairs. It was cramped; Jim was pleased to know that Beda had reserved four seats around a low table for the group. The stage was small with seating for the audience clustered close; a bar was situated just outside the main room. Decoration consisted of pictures of what Jim supposed must be jazz 'greats' on the walls and – bizarrely – beer crates were fixed to the ceiling – bottom up. Perhaps they improved the acoustics or provided sound proofing, Jim mused.

As expected the band only arrived at 9:45 and didn't start playing until about 10, by which time the room was already filled with cigarette smoke and a second round of beers had been ferried from the bar.

'So what's the name of the sax player you mentioned?' Jim enquired of Irena.

'Hans Dulfer, a strange name but as I said, he is Dutch.'

After the first set, the band took a break and conversation again became possible. Jim wondered how the musicians could manage with all the smoke in the room; he was finding breathing uncomfortable even though he was not playing a wind instrument.

Roger leaned toward Irena and asked if she knew the name of the club Dulfer was said to be managing in Amsterdam. Irena exchanged a few words with an acquaintance seated nearby, then replied, 'Paradiso, it's called Paradiso.'

Roger and Irena then fell into conversation. Jim however found himself staring, fascinated at a lonely figure propped up against the bar, occasionally sipping at his beer. The man was slim, Jim judged him to be about 30 years old with straggly shoulder length hair, wearing a leather jacket, faded and frayed jeans, and 'cowboy-style' boots. He was dressed like a student but obviously was not. His eyes and demeanour gave the impression he was thinking of a tragedy witnessed in the past.

Beda noticed Jim's fixation and remarked, 'That's Josef Koudelka, he gives lectures in photography at the Institute and appears in productions with a local theatre group from time to time. I took his class last semester, he is passionate about his subject, believes photography has the power to change attitudes as well as inform. Come, allow me to introduce you. He speaks a little English and loves to meet foreigners. We need to buy another round anyway.'

'Hello Josef, this is Jim Cricket, he is visiting us from England. Jim is Gerald Bond's nephew, that is to say the son of Gerald's sister.'

Koudelka straighten up, his face suddenly alive, he shook Beda's hand briefly then turned to Jim and warmly shook his hand. 'Gerald's relation, good, I often sit at back of Gerald's class to add to my vo... vo...'

'Vocabulary' interjected Jim helpfully, 'it is an immense pleasure to meet you Josef. Beda just told me that your photographs of Gypsies and contributions to the Prague theatre magazine are making you famous. Congratulations.'

'It's an exaggeration; I am only an ex-engineer with a weekend camera.' Koudelka replied modestly. 'The theatre magazine gives a little money, helps to pay for film and the needs of life.'

'Allow me to buy you a beer Josef. I hope we will meet again, good luck with your photography.' As Jim completed this sentence the band struck up again, making conversation impossible. Beda took four beer bottles by the neck, two in each hand and headed back to their table, Jim paid, handed Josef his beer, shook hands with him and followed.

The friends parted at the tram stop in Spálená at about 3am. The early glow of the approaching sunrise was touching the sky as Roger and Jim finally entered Gerald's apartment. Gentle snoring emanating from their host's room indicated he was home as they prepared for bed as quietly as possible. Unfortunately in the unusual silence of the early hour the flat's plumbing made an ear jarring noise, loud enough to wake the dead, or so it seemed to Jim, but to his relief the rhythm of the snoring did not change.

Chapter 9

Prague 1968 August

Surfacing from slumber at around noon on Sunday, Jim and Roger found a note from Gerald on the dining table; "Dinner this evening cancelled, sorry, urgent duties. Need you to take care of yourselves for time being, explore, and have fun. I'll see you when I see you. Gerald".

Since they already felt quite 'at home' in Prague, Gerald's missive was well received by Jim and Roger. Other than notes and signs that he had been in the apartment at some point Sunday and Monday, they did not see Gerald. However on Tuesday at about 8am they were woken by Kinia banging on their door. Gerald was on the phone, wanting to speak with Jim urgently.

'James, no questions now, I'm sending the car in half an hour, to collect both of you. Pack your things; you will be staying in a guest room at the Embassy for the rest of your visit. I'll explain later.'

They approached the British Embassy, at Thunovská 180/14, along a short, narrow cobbled street blocked at the far end by three storey wall that appeared to be a gate house of sorts. The Union Flag was in evidence to clearly mark United Kingdom territory. The larger door in the centre opened to permit their car to proceed into a rectangular parking area; to the right it was enclosed by what they took to be the rear wall of a neighbouring building. Ahead a three story building that had the appearance of a grand residence adjoined the Embassy, which stood four stories tall to their left. The Embassy's white wall assaulted their eyes as it harshly reflected the sun's rays. The building sparkled as the sun caught some of the sash windows that pierced the wall, which was set under a red tiled roof.

The reception area looked out on a large park that hugged the castle ramparts at the rear of the Embassy. The well-kept terraced lawns dusted with early autumn leaf fall, the pond replete with fountain and the mature trees dressed in autumn hues of rust-red, gold and brown leaves presented a restful vista to the eye.

They were shown to their quarters immediately, where they left their luggage. Then they were ushered into an anteroom, where they were left with instructions to wait for Gerald. The whole building seemed abuzz with activity, and both young men felt the nerves of their stomach tighten – so called 'butterflies' – as the tension in the air was palpable.

Roger fidgeted with some publications on a table beside his seat, as they waited. He chanced upon a description of the Embassy, which he read aloud in an effort to calm his nerves.

"The Embassy occupies the Thun Palace, a handsome and historic building, situated in the heart of the Malá Strana or "Little Quarter". The long history of the site goes back to medieval times and there are Gothic traces in the cellars and foundations of the building. The first written record of a building at this place is from the middle of the 14th Century. Since then, the location has marked some of the great events in Czech history. There are records that a house here was burnt during the Hussite wars, along with much of Malá Strana. Rudolf Second bequeathed a rebuilt house to one of his faithful servants, and the house was subsequently traded by winners and losers during the catastrophic upheavals of the Thirty Years War.

It was one of the assassins of the great general of the Thirty Years War, Wallenstein, the Scottish adventurer Count Leslie, who sold it to the Thun family in 1656, after whom the building is now named and who owned it for 269 years. Originally from the South Tyrol, the Thuns became embroiled in the Thirty Years War, and, being on the winning side, profited greatly from them."

'Thank you for that fascinating walk through history Roger,' remarked Jim, with more than a hint of sarcasm in his voice. Mercifully Gerald entered the room at that moment, sharply jerking them into the present.

'Welcome gentlemen, apologies for my absence the last two days, and the clandestine call this morning. Kindly read these copies of the Official Secrets Act and, if so willing, sign the undertaking appended.'

That being done, Gerald resumed his discourse. 'Good, now I can bring you 'inside' in respect of confidential information. In his dispatch today - FCO 28/69 – our Ambassador in Moscow, Sir Geoffrey Harrison, informed London, I quote: "if there is one thing of which we can be sure it is that the Soviet leadership will spare no effort to bring down Mr Dubcek and all he stands for." End quote.'

Let me just add that the situation is looking very serious; we suspect that the Soviets will choose some form of military intervention. Hence my request that you move into the relative safety of the Embassy compound and remain here for the time being. Your parents would not forgive me should any misfortune befall you.

Having signed the undertaking you are free to venture beyond the visitor areas into those reserved for authorised personnel. Here are your personal passes, please wear them at all times. I suggest you observe what is likely to be tragic history in the making from this vantage point, but don't interrupt or distract any member of staff going about their important work. The canteen and the library are of course available to feed your body and mind. Now I must leave you, if you have questions of a domestic nature, I suggest you ask June Green, the lady who showed you to your quarters earlier. She is usually to be found at Reception.'

'Thank you Gerald!' Jim and Roger chorused as he left the room.

At about 10:50pm Jim and Roger were chatting with a couple of off-duty communications officers over mugs of tea, having enjoyed a student friendly snack of baked beans on toast. Suddenly a commotion was heard in the corridor and a man entered, as the room fell silent instinctively, he announced with an unmistakable urgency in his voice; 'Everyone to their stations now, Soviet troops have taken over the airport, looks like the precursor of a full-fledged invasion!'

Sure enough light tanks of the Russian army were reported to be rolling down Leninova Avenue at 4am. There had been no resistance as the initial force took up positions in the city. It was soon learned that the Warsaw Pact was committing at least 200,000 troops to the expedition. In order to avoid bloodshed, the Czech government ordered its armed forces not to resist the invasion. However when the people woke to the realisation that the Soviets were intent on turning back the tentative reforms recently instituted; students, academics, business executives, all classes of society took every opportunity over the 21st and 22nd to attack the invaders with crude weapons – such as bricks and stones – and to protest. Streets were blockaded; ammunition trucks and tanks were reported to have been destroyed. As youths threw home-made missiles, Soviet troops responded with machinegun and artillery fire. Reports of the numbers of people killed by the invaders varied, and there was no way for them to be verified by Embassy staff. The invaders announced a night curfew and threatened to shoot anyone ignoring the order. Road, rail and airline routes out of Czechoslovakia were closed as the rest of the invasion force continued to pour into the country.

The Embassy fell silent late in the day to listen to a statement by US President Johnson, read over the Tannoy system.

"The tragic news from Czechoslovakia shocks the conscience of the world. The Soviet Union and its allies have invaded a defenceless country to stamp out a resurgence of ordinary human freedom. It is a sad commentary on the Communist mind that a sign of liberty in Czechoslovakia is deemed a fundamental threat to the security of the Soviet system. The excuses by the Soviet Union are patently contrived. The Czechoslovakian Government did not request its allies to interfere in its internal affairs. No external aggression threatened Czechoslovakia... in the name of mankind's hope for peace, I call on the Soviet Union and its associates to withdraw their troops from Czechoslovakia. I hope responsible spokesmen for governments and people throughout the world will support this appeal. It is never too late for reason to prevail."

Jim and Roger were only able to glean titbits of information during the hours that followed, however on the 22nd a copy of a telegram sent by the Ambassador, Sir William Barker, to the Foreign Office, describing the aftermath of the invasion was pinned to the staff notice board. The Embassy's agents had been out on the streets and contacts throughout the city had been calling to report, all at great risk to their safety. The Ambassador summarised the situation as follows:

"At 10.00 hours today the situation in Prague is on the surface calmer. This is due presumably to the consolidation of Soviet Control on the outskirts of the city, artillery and anti-aircraft guns are dug within. The squares in which the people tend to rally are completely commanded by tanks, infantry and anti-aircraft weapons. The road to, but not from, the airport is barred by Soviet tanks but the bridges are almost all free and movement is comparatively easy

There are lots of people in the streets especially in Vaclavske Square. Some are wearing anti-Soviet placards on their backs – young people are still driving around in cars with Czechoslovak flags and placards. 'Go home!' and similar inscriptions are still going up. Newspapers including since yesterday evening a new one called 'Freedom' and all unmistakeably pro- Dubcek are being distributed from quick moving vehicles... One's conclusion is that the Occupiers have total text book military control but that the population as yet are showing no signs of reconciling themselves to the situation."

Gerald, looking exhausted and in desperate need of a shower, joined his nephew and friend in the canteen that evening. 'Well gentlemen the Bear arrived expecting a brief skirmish with Czechoslovak forces, a welcome from the people and resignation of the government. Instead they met no formal resistance, an outpouring or opprobrium from the people, who are now more united behind their government than ever before, and an administration that continues to function. They are confused to say the least. Nevertheless the invasion is a tragic turn of events and the loss of life heart-breaking.'

'Do you have any news of Irena, Beda and Kinia,' enquired Roger.

'Yes they are fine. I suggested they all stay in my flat, which they sensibly did, as far as I know. You may call them yourself to check.'

In the following days it was learnt that the Czech and Slovak people had heard the call of many of their number to unite in non-violent protest. Several mobile broadcast stations were in operation, keeping the local population informed. Apparently the invading forces had been told to expect to be welcomed by the populace, so were taken aback when spat upon and verbally abused by passers-by; ranging from students, to public officials, office workers and mothers. Their tanks were being painted with swastikas when stopped at traffic lights.

Street and direction signs throughout the country were painted out, and many villages changed their names to Dubcek or Svoboda, making it difficult for the invaders to find their way about the cities and country. Soviet troops occupying Bratislava Castle found the water cut-off. Having brought only powder rations they had to set off in search of water in order to satisfy their hunger. Strangely they found that there was no water available in homes or buildings and, having been warned that water from the public tap had been poisoned by "counter-revolutionaries", some resorted to sourcing water from puddles or the Danube, only to fall ill.

Graffiti appeared everywhere with slogans such as; "Why bother to occupy our State Bank? You know there is nothing in it" and "An elephant cannot swallow a hedgehog".

It was reported that in Eastern Bohemia local citizens formed a human chain across a bridge and blockaded a Russian convoy of tanks and other vehicles. After eight and a half hours the Russians turned back.

On August 26, at 9am, Czechoslovakians throughout the country made noise; church bells rang, car horns sounded, sirens and train whistles blew. The din frightened some of the occupying troops – many were young conscripts. In Klarov a woman was shot as a result. The noise was followed by a one-hour general strike, effective throughout the country.

That evening Gerald announced that it would be possible for Jim and Roger to leave on a flight being arranged by the British government to evacuate its citizens, the following afternoon.

'I suggest you walk down to the flat in the morning and spend time with Irena and Beda, Kinia will make you lunch so you can have a 'relaxed' conversation. I will come in the Embassy car, with your luggage, to pick you up at 2pm and escort you to the airport.'

'Thank you Gerald, we were worried we wouldn't be able to say proper farewells to our new friends.'

Roger continued, 'It has been a really strange ten day visit, such a stark contrast between the carefree sunny days before the invasion and the overcast dark days since. I'm full of admiration for the Czechoslovak people. Their solidarity, fortitude and imaginative non-violent protest tactics.....just awe inspiring!

A subdued Kinia greeted them at the door when they arrived at the flat. Beda hurried into the room as soon as he heard their voices in the entrance. He greeted them warmly and explained that Irena was speaking to a friend on the phone so would join them soon. Her friend's brother had been badly injured during a protest demonstration in the first days of the invasion. Irena was checking on his condition and trying to comfort her friend.

'Before Irena joins us, come into the bedroom. Roger, please close the door.' Beda continued with a conspiratorial tone, as he began to explain himself. 'I met Josef last night, Josef Koudelka.'

'The photographer?' interjected Jim, seeking confirmation.

'Yes, the photographer. Josef has been taking photographs night and day since the invasion began. He has literally taken thousands. They are an important record of what has happened this past week. He is desperate to have these pictures reach the western world. He entrusted them to me in the hope that you would consent to take them to London. I must warn you that this is a dangerous undertaking. The Soviet occupiers, curse them, are taking every possible measure to stop this sort of evidence leaving the country. Josef's name as the photographer must never be attributed, or he would surely face imprisonment or worse. Are you gentlemen willing to smuggle these photos out when you leave today?'

'Yes!' Immediately they both answered in unison.

'Good. Don't tell Gerald, we don't want the Embassy implicated in any way. Please deliver them to a photographic agency called 'Magnum' in London. The photos can be published but not credited, only anonymously published. Impress upon them that the photographer's name must not – *must not* – be revealed under any circumstances.'

'We understand.' Jim responded. 'As well as a great responsibility, it is a great honour to do this small task to help the cause of peace and freedom for the people of Czechoslovakia.'

When Gerald arrived Jim and Roger were permitted to secrete their farewell 'gifts' in their luggage, after explaining that they already had too much 'carry-on' baggage. To their surprise and delight they found that their suitcases were marked "Diplomatic Bag". When queried, Gerald retorted, with a broad grin; 'There's no way some Soviet snoop is going to be permitted to go through your dirty laundry, while you are my responsibility!'

After tearful farewells and fraternal hugs all round, shame Kinia was particularly upset, they piled into the Embassy car and headed to the airport. En route Jim teased; 'Roger, the hug you shared with Irena seemed a might more than a fraternal politeness!'

'Well she is a very nice person.' Roger retorted, as a grin spread across his blushing face. 'We exchanged addresses, so intend to stay in touch, the postal service permitting.'

'Hmm, I love it when a plan comes together!' Gerald interjected, indicating that he may have had a hidden agenda when he chose Irena as one of the pair to host his guests.

Needless to say, with Gerald at their side, all the way through the exit formalities at the airport, replete with courier accreditations and the necessary manifest, Roger and Jim met no difficulty. With their 'Diplomatic Bags' safely stowed in the hold they waited while other passengers endured the inconvenience of having luggage searched for 'security reasons'. Then, as the plane door closed Gerald gave a cheery wave from the tarmac, turned on heel and strode into the airport building. Simultaneously the plane was pushed back, turned and began to taxi towards the run-way.

Chapter 10

London 1990 February

'Hello Jim! What are you staring at? You were gazing out the window when I passed your office twenty minutes ago. Don't you have any work to do?' Jenny teased as she breezed into his office.

'Jenny, good morning, I was just reminiscing about the ten days I spent in Prague nearly 22 years ago. That reminds me that I haven't written to my friend Beda for a while, I should do so this evening. So, how are you this morning?'

'I'm fine! I have an interesting, or I should say worrisome case to report.   Payables referred an unpaid invoice to me yesterday. It's for over $300,000 and has been outstanding for more than six weeks.'

'Payables? Why Payables, surely they pay supplier invoices, they don't issue invoices?'

'Yes, that is part of the problem. We purchased a cargo of LPG, you know Liquefied Petroleum Gas, from a Greek trading company.   Our Traders, being very aware of the need to neutralise price risk, negotiated a pricing formula to match the pricing they had already agreed with the ultimate buyer. Well Market Risk was perfectly hedged, that is we were contracted to pay for and receive from the sale of the cargo the Average of Platts quoted prices over the month of December, minus a small discount on the purchase side and plus a small premium on the sale.'

'Business as usual, so what went wrong?'

'The Payment Terms! The Greek company was short of cash, so Trading in their wisdom negotiated an additional 'cost of funds' discount in return for agreeing to pay for the cargo '5 days after Bill of Lading date' based on a preliminary invoice, with a 'true-up' final invoice settlement five days after the month end.

The cargo loaded on December 12, so Payables accepted the Greek's preliminary invoice based on the average price over the prior 20 trading days. Unfortunately they did not consult our Traders, or look at the price trend at the time. The price dropped sharply early December and remained low. Hence a recalculation later, based on the December average, revealed we had over paid handsomely.'

'Ah...and they haven't refunded the excess! Ouch! Obviously we must tighten up the commodity purchase side of our business, but why has it taken so long to be brought to your notice?'

'Our colleagues in Payables did not have an appreciation of the fact that the longer a debt is unpaid the more unlikely we are to collect. In short they tried to sort this out themselves without the necessary sense of urgency. They first requested the Greeks to issue a final invoice reflecting the correct price and to refund our overpayment. Two weeks passed with no response to the initial request or follow up faxes. Then Payables issued our invoice requesting payment upon receipt and faxed it to Athens. The Christmas and New Year period caused delays in action. Do you know that the Greeks and Russians celebrate Christmas on January 7; it's December 25th according to the Julian calendar? So that was a reason to excuse a lack of response without raising the alarm, but here we are mid-February and still no reply from Athens'

'So what is your action plan?'

'Well, I contacted John K, our marine lubricant distributor in Piraeus, and asked him to investigate Phoenix Trading EPE. It's a limited liability company. According to the Compliance file there are two director shareholders.

John sent someone to the address we have on record for Phoenix. He reported that there is a trading business operating at the premises but the new looking name plate announces "Success Trading EPE". Subsequently John called the phone number our Traders used for Phoenix. The person who answered explained that Phoenix has ceased trading, Success has taken over. When he asked to speak to the

Directors of Phoenix by name, John was put on hold, then told one was out and the other would return his call when free. Needless to say John's call has not been returned.

John has recommended the partner of a local law firm. So I called him and he confirmed he will be happy to act for ShamOil in this case. I followed up with a fax asking him to establish the standing of Phoenix and obtain financial statements if available, so we can decide how to proceed.'

'Good, you obviously have the problem in hand. What do you want me to do?'

'Nothing at the moment, but I will need your support in negotiating procedural changes necessary to ensure we, in Credit, review all potential commodity suppliers in future. We will also have to vet the payment and adequate assurance terms in every commodity purchase contract before it is finalised. Oh, if we need a face to face meeting with the Directors of Phoenix, can I count on you to support me in person?'

'Of course, you can always count on me to support you in person, especially when it means a visit to Athens. If we are lucky the Acropolis guards won't be on strike when we visit this time, so we will be able to visit the Parthenon.

Speaking of foreign travel, when and where is the next credit conference scheduled to take place?'

'The next is an FCIB conference that will take place in Vienna, early June.'

'FCIB?'

'Yes, it was a mystery to me and the acronym is not particularly meaningful, so I did some digging. It is an association of professionals involved in Finance Credit and International Business. Started in the US for credit professionals working with exporting companies, it now has an active Europe wide membership coordinated by an executive in the UK.'

'Hmm, Vienna, I haven't been there, I suppose the conference will be focussing on the implications of the Wall having come down for West-East trade and credit risk. Oh, by the way Oily has asked Simon to arrange lunch-time Russian language lessons for anyone interested. Will you sign up?'

'I don't know, I will have to give it thought, seems like a great opportunity but I'm already taking French lessons on Saturday mornings. You know how passionate language teachers are, they always pile on the homework, I'm not sure I could handle two languages at the same time.'

'I expect it will be several weeks before lessons commence so you don't have to decide immediately. Before I forget, please give me a copy of the Single Name Credit Insurance presentation we saw at the Dublin conference.'

'Okay, but what happened to your copy and why the sudden interest?'

'You know I don't like to keep paper. Simon almost bumped into me in the corridor on my way in this morning, he mentioned, that our Traders will be tendering to supply refined product to Nigeria in the coming months. I remember Roger telling me that the Nigerians always pay late – although they always pay and even pay interest eventually – and the few banks that provide 'silent' cover tend to reserve their limited capacity for regular clients, namely the big trading houses.'

'So you are thinking that we may have to tap the insurance market in order to cover any product sales? We could retain some of the risk but definitely not 100%, California will certainly not approve a completely open line to begin with, and when they see delayed payments they'll freak out!'

'Yes, exactly, and being new to the business we are unlikely to be able to find bank capacity available if we win a cargo. On the other hand Simon will not want to pay to reserve capacity that he will not use if we don't win a tender. This will be an interesting challenge; a good opportunity for you to add value,' Jim said with a broad smile lighting up his face.

He continued, 'I would like to meet with the Lloyds of London Broker who made the presentation. I figure I should read his presentation first though 'cause I admit I didn't pay much attention when he was speaking.'

'Right, I'll give you a copy later today and contact Finlay Finlayson to make an appointment for us to meet. I have a few questions to ask him so I look forward to the opportunity.'

After reading through the copies of the presentation transparencies after lunch, Jim noted some questions that came to mind, then 'filed' the paper.

Chapter 11

London 1990 June

'Hello Jenny! Welcome to Lloyds!' Finlay Finlayson enthused, greeting Jenny as she cleared security screening and entered the iconic headquarters of Lloyds of London in Lime Street. 'And you must be James Cricket?' said Finlay, turning to Jim and shaking his hand.

'Yes, it is good to meet you Finlay. Sorry we didn't actually meet in Dublin but I did attend your presentation. I was obviously intrigued since here we are, at the heart of insurance. Thank you for meeting us here, I've walked past many times, also admired the building from afar, but never ventured inside.'

'Good, that is good to hear because I've arranged for a quick visit to the in-house museum and a mini-tour to set the background for our discussions.'

On the third level, as they wondered through the museum, Jenny remarked, 'Wow, so this all started in a coffee shop in 1688, Lloyd's Coffee House. I'm fascinated to learn that Lloyd was the owner of the coffee shop, not an insurer but the founder, or more correctly the facilitator, of the marine insurance business. I've heard about the Lutine Bell, is it still somewhere in the building, is it still rung when a ship is lost at sea?' Jenny was becoming a little 'tipsy' drinking at the cup of the history that pervaded the building, despite its futuristic appearance.

'The bell still hangs in the Rostrum. That's the beautiful wooden structure you can see in the midst of the Atrium, the Underwriting Room, down there,' Finlay replied pointing out a tall, elegant edifice that dominated the large rectangular floor space of the Atrium. It was flanked along each side of the room by rows of desks, at which mainly men in suits and ties, variously sat poring over papers held in manila folders, chatted in small groups, or dashed about delivering or collecting files. The Rostrum was topped by a very impressive two sided, analogue clock. At one end of the Atrium escalators continuously rolled up and down respectively, connecting the Atrium to the upper floors, which appeared to be a series of open galleries. Gazing down at all the sober suited ladies and gentlemen, Jim fingered his tie. He was not accustomed to wearing a tie, having abandoned the practice when he left banking and moved into the commercial trading environment, but he had been warned that "jacket and tie" was de rigueur dress for any man visiting Lloyds.

'Sadly the bell will no longer be rung because it has developed a crack. The decision to end the tradition was made only last year, after the arrival of an overdue ship caused it to be rung twice. The Lutine was traditionally rung once for a lost ship – bad news – and twice for the arrival of an overdue – good news.'

'How long was that the practice?

'Well it was recovered from the wreck in 1858 but I'm not sure when exactly it was hung in the Underwriting Room of that time. I guess it had to be cleaned up so if it has been functioning since, say 1859. About 131 years!'

'Finlay, I notice that any walls are glass and even the escalators are encased in glass, so we can watch the inner mechanism churning, the lifts too are transparent. What inspired the architect?' piped up Jim, with a sudden burst of curiosity.

'Well it was Richard Rogers' way of expressing the insurance concept of "uberrimae fidei" – utmost good faith – which is basically about transparency. The inside-out design of the exterior of the building is also an expression of that concept. The point is that the Underwriters share risks; by marking a file with the percentage of any loss they will cover and their signature, as the file passes from desk to desk, so they have to trust that the file contains all the information available. Likewise the syndicates of Underwriters are taking on customer's risks largely on the basis of the description of the risk provided by the insured. Therefore if an insured lied or omitted vital risk affecting facts the insurer will repudiate the contract on grounds that the insured did not provide information in utmost good faith.'

'Finlay, surely Underwriters do their own research and analysis?' Jim retorted in amazement.

'Well some Underwriters, particularly those interested in taking risk in emerging markets have recently set up research departments, but most rely on the insured's risk management and full disclosure – the insured's due diligence – as the basis for their decision. That and the ability to repudiate a claim should it turn out that vital information was withheld.'

'Not to cast aspersions but in the outside world, that is known as an insurer's "wriggle room". Some believe that an insurer can wriggle out of its commitment to pay a claim like an escapologist can wriggle out of a straitjacket; thanks to all the "ifs, buts and uberrima fides" in the purposely boring policy document.'

'Yes, but it is in the power of the insured to avoid rejected claims by means of good, open and frequent communication. That's where your broker comes into the picture, as an adviser and go-between. Let's adjourn to the pub downstairs where we can discuss this in comfort.'

As the trio made their way to street level, Finlay and Jenny chatted amiably. Jim tagged along a couple of paces behind them, deep in thought. He had just come to the realisation that it was the insurers' unfunded risk-taking business model that had spawned the wealth that was exuded by the building and financial status of the people in the industry. Roger had mentioned that silent guarantees covering NNPC credit risk were being charged at 500 basis points per annum. Five percent earned on zero investment, in fact any amount earned on zero equals an infinite return. A truly great business model provided one can avoid major losses, which Jim felt one could surely do in the case of credit risk, with the application of some astute analysis and assessment.

Once in the lift Jim could no longer zone out the conversation. Finlay had apparently just enquired about Jenny's absence from work the previous week.

'We spent the week in Mallorca with two couples; the six of us take a "city break" together at the end of May each year. Usually we are away only three nights, but given the extra travel time involved with this destination we decided to lengthen the stay."

'Really, Mallorca, from what I've heard of Mallorca I wouldn't think it would suit a refined person such as you.'

'That was my reaction when the visit was first mooted, but we didn't stay in Palma. We took a taxi direct to Soyea – that's spelt "Sóller" – the double "l" in Spanish is pronounced "ye". Well Sóller is a lovely small village, quiet with a sedate lifestyle and some good restaurants. The visit was so restful, many hours sitting in the shade at a café on the town square, sipping a cool drink and people watching. It was a magical week, very relaxing.'

'Talking of sipping cool drinks,' said Finlay as they reached the Corney & Barrow that nestled under a wing of the main building, at street level. 'What can I order for you?'

'A hot chocolate for me, no cream; I'll be driving home from the station this evening.'

Jim scanned the drinks menu on the table and ventured, 'I'll be walking home from the station this evening so I'll risk a glass of the Shiraz Cabernet, thanks.'

Soon they were settled around a table in one corner of the pub. It was early evening so they were able to sit some distance away from the only other patrons, who also appeared to be having a business meeting rather than a social gathering.

'Thank you Finlay,' said Jim, acknowledging the 250ml of velvet red liquid that was delivered. 'Cheers! Sláinte! Before Jenny launches into her list of technical questions, please clarify for me your role as a broker; for example, how are you paid?'

'I'm happy to do that Jim. The broker fee is allocated from the premium paid by the insured, ShamOil in this case. The payment is actually made by the insurer but I represent and assist the insured, ShamOil.

My role is to interpret your, ShamOil's, needs into the language and ultimately the policy text that is understood and accepted by the insurance market. I have to explain the terms and conditions to you, and explain to the lead insurer your reasoning for taking insurance. Therefore I need to understand what is motivating ShamOil to shift its risk onto the market; as well as your history and your experience in dealing with the NNPC in this case. So I'm afraid I will have to ask a lot of questions and rely on you to provide me with all pertinent information.

Once the policy is in place I will communicate details of the individual deals that you wish to be covered under the policy, from time to time. I will remind you when premium payments become due and review your information updates then pass them onto the lead underwriter. Generally my role is to make sure that you do not overlook any of the conditions and/or warranties undertaken in the policy. I will also handle any advice of delayed payment, receipt of payments, and any claims you may register.'

'So you are really a key link between the underwriting fraternity and their customers, the insured. That's very helpful, thank you. Jenny?'

Taking her cue from Jim, Jenny said with a smile, 'Sorry this seems like an interrogation Finlay, but we're taking our first tentative steps into this, to us, still murky world.

Since we were told to expect to manage NNPC credit risk, I've spoken to a couple of banks, to feel out their appetite and try to agree documentation in advance of an opportunity. In the commodity trading business Traders are for the most part opportunists so when they see an opportunity they expect Credit to respond instantly. On the other hand they very seldom have a strategy so it is difficult for us to prepare. Jim's phrase for our challenge is "leading from behind", which I interpret to mean having to anticipate which counterparties Traders may deal with, and making advance plans to be in a position to provide a prompt answer to the question; "I have a prospective deal with X the only buyer out there, I need to close the deal in half an hour, what are the credit terms?"

In the highly competitive world of commodity trading it is not always possible to simply answer "fully secured by Letter of Credit opened or confirmed by an acceptable bank". Either our competitors have done their homework and offer open terms on the basis of their assessment of the credit worthiness of the counterparty, or they are prepared with access to banks willing to sell them silent – that is undisclosed – payment guarantees.

On the other hand most National Oil companies, like NNPC, simply refuse to provide collateral so we have to be prepared to give open account terms. To the extent that we can't accept the full amount of potential exposure we have to lay-off the risk. At least in the case of NNPC we have been given warning of our Traders' plans.'

'Indeed, I'm pleased to know that you are planning ahead,' Finlay offered. 'It takes four to six weeks to set up a new policy. Once the policy is in place individual deals can be covered instantly, and you know in advance that any deal within the policy definition will be covered. Policies usually provide that "the Insurer is permitted to cancel this policy on the grounds of (a) non-payment of premium in accordance with the agreement or (b) the insolvency of the Insured", which means you can be confident committing to provide open account for say six cargoes delivered monthly over the next six months.'

'That will be very comforting Finlay,' Jim interjected, 'because the bank's seem to have limited appetite individually and, from all accounts, it is being rationed on a first come first served basis or withheld for use by certain favoured clients. So we fear that, if we rely on the banks we could win a tender then find no bank cover available. My boss would not be happy if we were to carry 100% of a cargo unsecured, especially with delayed payment being the norm in this case.'

'The insurance market certainly has an advantage in that respect Jim. It is very deep and broad, and the syndicate underwriting process not only shares the risk, it also enables the whole risk appetite of the market to be accessed.'

'But what about the cost, your presentation mentioned a minimum premium,' mused Jenny. 'We have to allocate the cost of silent cover to transactions. Traders are ever watchful of their "bonus pool", I wonder how we would sell the idea of credit insurance to them?'

'The minimum premium is negotiable down to a point, but it certainly will be an important aspect for you and your Traders to consider. I will talk to a potential lead underwriter — if they are interested they should indicate the expected premium and minimum. How much exposure do you expect to need to cover and what percentage would you need to cover?'

'I have some rough numbers Finlay. Each cargo would be about 500,000 barrels. There is not much mark-up on the crude oil price, even though refineries add most of the value the production end captures most of the profit, so say US$15 million per delivery, on risk from NOR for up to 120 days. On that basis our exposure would peak in the fourth month at about $60 million, depending on the timing of deliveries within each month. To be on the safe side we must work on basis of a five cargo overlap, since the fifth may be on the water before we realise that payment for the first is delayed beyond 120 days. Although we are confident our banking contacts would advise us if they noticed any slippage in the payment pattern in respect of invoices due to other suppliers. We have ShamOil staff resident in Nigeria, so we will also ask them to visit with NNPC to check the progress of our invoices, apparently they would need to be signed by several officials and would then be batched for payment with others.'

'Okay, I've noted a peak exposure of around $75 million, building up over four months with invoices outstanding up to 120 days. However on the phone you mentioned that the contract terms are "30 days after NOR", what is "NOR" by the way?'

'Oh sorry, I should have explained, NOR stands for "Notice of Readiness to dock and discharge or load the cargo". When a ship is within a few hours of arriving at its destination port the Master initiates a telex message addressed to the Port Authority stating his expected time of arrival and requesting a suitable berth. The NOR is copied to the seller and buyer of the product or goods on-board. The time of despatch of the NOR starts the clock running on the period allowed in the sell/buy contract for the ship to be in port, so if there is a delay demurrage can be calculated. Demurrage is charged or calculated per day so any delay increases the shipping cost. The extra cost is usually to be paid by the party at fault, so either the seller or the buyer, therefore records like the NOR are important. "Demurrage" is compensation paid for causing a delay in loading or discharging a ship.'

'I see; thanks. Actually I don't understand why Nigeria imports refined product when it produces and exports so much crude oil, and why the delayed payments considering the vast amounts of US dollars earned from profit and taxes on the crude oil it exports?'

Finlay had addressed Jim when posing these questions, anxious not to leave him out of the conversation, but Jim merely looked at Jenny, who continued. 'Unfortunately due to poor maintenance over many years the refineries in Nigeria operate at low utilisation rates and only sporadically. Yes the export of crude oil brings substantial amounts of foreign currency into Nigerian government coffers but as more or less the only source of revenue there are many competing demands on the funds. Allocation of the actual cash flow is therefore subject to prioritisation and bureaucratic controls.'

At this point Jim felt he should chip in to give Jenny an opportunity to savour her now sufficiently cooled hot chocolate. 'Yes, the availability of a stream of US dollars combined with the history of civil strife – rioting, burning and looting – whenever filling stations have run dry in the past, are the reasons petroleum products have always been paid for in the past, and why we are sanguine about being paid for our deliveries in the future.'

'This is all tremendously helpful information,' Finlay remarked, looking up from his notebook. 'So why doesn't ShamOil avoid the cost of a silent guarantee of political risk insurance altogether, why buy insurance? The lead underwriter will definitely want to be assured that he is not taking on a risk you believe is going to go bad.'

'That is exactly the question on the lips of our Traders!' Jenny exclaimed.

'The reason is that we already have considerable exposure to NNPC, in respect of our upstream operations.' Jim continued, 'ShamOil and other major international oil companies operate Nigerian oil fields, the pipeline networks, the terminals and the floating storage vessels, but in every case in partnership with NNPC.

Consequently, when the partners agree to invest money upgrading infrastructure or extending a field NNPC has to pay its share of the cost. The operating company, ShamOil in our case, goes ahead with the investment and bills its partners for their share. As a result ShamOil carries some very hefty receivables from NNPC, adding petroleum product receipts could push us past our "single name" maximum exposure limit!' Jim paused, as his use of the term "single name" in the alternative context of corporate concentration risk brought a smile to the lips of the trio.

'We are willing to retain up to $15 million so we may be able to carry more than the minimum 10% required by underwriters, in respect of some individual cargoes. That would enable us to average down the cost of insurance on a per barrel basis.'

'Yes, to that point,' Jenny interjected. 'I've not been happy with the wording of some of the silent bank guarantees I've reviewed.'

'What aspects in particular?' Finlay enquired.

'Well I see the arrangement as a "risk sharing" joint venture, but some aspects are one-way in favour of the bank. For example, recoveries go first to pay off the bank then when the bank is fully paid anything else collected comes to us. Recovery costs are also unevenly shared. We could not accept such an arrangement so I hope we can negotiate a more balanced approach with the lead underwriter.

I've drafted this text for inclusion in a guarantee or policy to illustrate what we would like to see, this is based on a guarantee,' Jenny continued handing two printed A4 sheets to Finlay and a copy to Jim. 'You will see that recoveries, for instance, are shared on the basis of the risk share. Hence if ShamOil retains 30% of an invoice then 30% of any related amount recovered comes to ShamOil, only the balance goes to the insurer.'

'That seems reasonable,' Finlay remarked, as he briefly scanned the draft. Jim stared absentmindedly at the page long enough, he judged, to give the impression of interest. In fact he was thinking about the amount of time that would be required to give administering an insurance programme due care and attention. It occurred to him that this and other recent developments required giving serious consideration to increasing the size of his team.

'Good, if that's all your questions, tomorrow I'll discuss this with Zurich Global Corporate; they are a leading underwriter of political risk and trade credit insurance for multinational companies and exporters. They also carry a good credit rating.

What about another drink?'

'This is my round Finlay,' retorted Jim as he folded the draft neatly and slipped it into the left inside pocket of his jacket. 'What's your pleasure?'

With that Jenny excused herself, shook hands with Finlay, and made her way home. Jim ordered two whiskeys, Glenfiddich single malt, 18 years old, and talked fondly of his visit to the distillery as a tourist several years previously. This launched a long and entirely convivial conversation around the highlights of visiting Scotland, which it turned out Jim and his wife had toured extensively.

FILE 13 – a.k.a. Jim's Paper Recycle Bin

The Dublin Presentation:
Strategic Credit Risk Management
Providing Solutions – Adding Value

Reasons to Grant Credit

Product Enhancement

In order to differentiate a product from similar competitor products a special credit term may be added to the product specification.

Examples are the offer of '0% financing', or 'no payments for a year and a day', or simply the offer of terms of '45 days after date of invoice' when competitors selling an otherwise similar product require cash paid in advance.

Comparative Cost of Money

If a supplier company has a credit rating superior to that of its customer, the cost of the working capital it must utilise to finance 'supplier credit' will be lower than the cost of the funds its buyer would have to borrow in order to pay promptly. Therefore a win-win opportunity arises.

In such a case the supplier could offer credit terms sufficient to cover (1) the period required by the buyer to sell the goods supplied, and (2) the time required to collect funds from the ultimate consumers. Hence the buyer would not have to borrow funds, avoiding bank interest costs, while the supplier would incur a comparatively low cost of funds. The net extra profit (as a result of a higher achievable price) could be retained by the seller, or shared between seller and buyer, through a price adjustment.

Administrative Efficiency

In many cases the cost of collecting cash in advance, in respect of many relatively small orders, will outweigh the risk of granting credit terms to an extent sufficient to permit monthly billing. In other cases the cost of issuing and administering numerous invoices will drive a decision to grant credit.

Comparative storage costs can also be an important consideration, in respect of this strategy. Manufacturers of agricultural fertiliser, for example, find it is cheaper to deliver fertiliser to farmers throughout the year rather than only delivering it just prior to the time it is needed. Farmer customers each build stocks of fertiliser close to their fields prior to use, instead of the manufacturer accumulating huge stockpiles remotely, and then delivering supplies to numerous farmers over a short period. The manufacturer reduces storage and transport costs in this way. However farmers are only able to pay for the fertiliser after selling their harvest, hence they require extended credit terms in order to accommodate this arrangement.

Building Trust

Credit is an excellent means through which to build trust into a seller-buyer relationship. Trust in the quality of the product and trust in the supplier's 'after-sales' service offer. Providing credit enables a seller to signal to a buyer that it has every confidence that the product will perform as promised, and that it wants to establish a long term relationship with the buyer. It also encourages the buyer to believe that the seller will not ignore any needs that the buyer may have for repair or replacement of faulty product after delivery.

Business Development

When a supplier wishes to assist a distributor (usually in an emerging market) to grow its business more quickly than the distributor's financial resources would normally allow, 'supplier credit' is a useful strategic tool.

Extended supplier credit will allow a distributor to recycle sales revenues collected (cash) within its domestic operations; to meet fixed expenses, finance its own receivables, and build necessary infrastructure as it expands.

Naturally such an arrangement must be closely managed, and calls for a high degree of trust on the supplier's side and transparency on the distributor's side.

....

PURPOSE

Nourishing Businesses... The Credit Team seeks to provide credit solutions that enhance internal and external customers' and suppliers' business models and sustainability.
The foundations for this work are:

- Compliance with Credit Policy,
- Holistic credit analysis,
- A "Yes; provided …. Can Do" attitude, and
- An on-going programme of research, development, participation in professional discussions, and networking.

VALUES
Integrity, Trust, Transparency, Creativity and Enterprise
In the event of conflict between these values, Integrity takes precedence. A decision based on Integrity is one that the decider would be proud to publish and defend.

VISION
Credit Team is an innovative, market leading, customer focused credit solutions provider - fully aligned with the Company's Strategic Intent. It is recognised as having great people with imagination, committed to delivering added value to internal and external customers. The team works 'as one'; guided by the values of integrity, trust, transparency, creativity and enterprise.

....

TWO TYPES OF CREDIT RISK

Performance Risk (Pre-Delivery Risk)
The risk a supplier or buyer will fail to honour a contract to supply or take delivery of goods at a future date. Potential loss measured by the additional cost, if any, of replacing the goods from another source (supplier failure) or selling the goods to another buyer (buyer failure).

Payment Risk (Post Delivery Risk)
The risk a buyer will fail to pay the invoiced amount for goods delivered, in full and/or on due date.

Due Diligence
The first priority before accepting any new customer or supplier (foreign or domestic) must be to ascertain whether it is a genuine business.

The full and correct name of the potential counterparty, its registered and main trading address(es) and the names of the owners or active executives must be established.

Independent opinion as to its reputation should be obtained.

....

The Art of B2B Credit Risk Assessment – An Introduction

People
People decide whether a business will perform or not, pay or not.

The Future
Risk management is about *Managing the Future*

The future is where businesses will perform or not, pay or not.

The future cannot be precisely predicted by reference to the past.

Means, Motivation and Opportunity to Perform and Pay

Means
Businesses are legal entities; they only exist in the imaginary legal sense.

Businesses are not balance sheets or income statements; they are collections of people working together.

Financial reports show where the business was and what it had; its last staging point.

Financial reports are easily and usually manipulated. Accounting rules allow numerous opportunities for management to show their results in the best light.

What is important is what the statements are not reporting and what they are hiding.

Poor management will cause a financially strong business to fail.

Good management can turn-around a financially weak business.

Nevertheless it is vital to assess if a counterparty will probably have the means to perform and pay in future. Use Forensic Cash Flow Analysis techniques.

Consider the Cash Flow Cycle to work out when cash will be available to pay i.e.:

(Days Inventory + Days Sales Outstanding) – Days Payables

Motivation – to Perform

Consider the ability of the buyer or supplier to maintain market share, in the event its competitors are able to source or sell a similar input commodity or finished good more cheaply or expensively, respectively.

A buyer may choose to repudiate a fixed price contract if it would become uncompetitive by purchasing inputs or finished goods at the contract price.

A supplier may choose to repudiate a fixed price contract should it be able to sell the commodity or finished good to other customers at a higher price.

A buyer or supplier may nevertheless choose to perform if, for example, (a) the commodity/good only forms a small portion of input costs or the contract quantity is a small portion of a seller's sales, or (b) the damage that would result to its reputation or relationship outweighs any possible short-term gain.

Also consider:

Availability of Stakeholder and/or Parent support

Political and/or social imperatives

Reputation and culture (business ethics)

Consequences for the counterparty (CP) of failure to perform

Legal consequences

Whether performance in some circumstances would threaten its survival

If the CP were to go into Administration (Chapter 11 equivalent) before performance or during a delivery period would the 'Administrator' continue the contract?

Motivation – to Pay

Post-delivery credit gives the buyer an 'option to default'.

Even if the buyer has the money to pay its management may decide not to pay.

On the other hand even if there is not enough money to pay all creditors its management may choose to pay you. Some examples of motivational factors are:

- The need to have a follow-up order delivered, and/or

- The need to protect the good name of the business; and thus to protect supplier credit obtained from other sources or to protect availability of bank credit

If a seller is considering a one-time-only sale or similar goods are available from many competitors, it may never receive its money. The buyer may be able to simply buy future supplies of the goods from someone else, after failing to pay.

Ultimately being paid or not, is a question of the 'balance of power' between the seller and the customer. Credit managers should weigh up the balance of power before approving delivery of an order on credit terms.

Opportunity to Perform

Consider the counterparty's business model and what relevant factors may change during the period between the contract agreement date and the delivery due date.

Create various stressed scenarios; consider the likely effect on the counterparty's situation and the likely outcome. For example, the market price of the goods changes unfavourably for the counterparty, but the counterparty holds a financial hedge therefore the negative effect is neutralised.

Opportunity to Pay

Conditions required to ensure a buyer has the opportunity to pay on due date, after delivery, include:

- Seller must provide accurate invoices and shipping documents promptly, and
- In the case of exports, the financial condition of the buyer's country must be good enough to permit the buyer to obtain the necessary currency remittance. If essential goods that cannot be obtained locally are involved, such as fuel, fertiliser, pharmaceuticals or food, related payments will usually be prioritised in the case of foreign currency shortages.

Conclusion

If you do not believe a potential customer has the means **and** the motive **and** the opportunity to pay on time, only authorise deliveries provided payment security is first obtained.

Note that most popular forms of payment or transfer risk security are not effective if the seller's administration fails to fully meet the terms of the security contract.

Types of payment or transfer risk security include; payment in advance, letters of credit (confirmed or not), bank guarantees, undisclosed risk sharing agreements or guarantees, Promissory Notes (avalised or not), Bankers' Acceptances, Parent Company Guarantees, Bank Payment Obligations and credit insurance.

Reminder

Risk cannot be eliminated, it must be managed. One way to manage risk is to transfer or transform it into an alternative form that is considered easier to control. Transaction related risk remains within the circle, flowing within the context of ever present global risks.

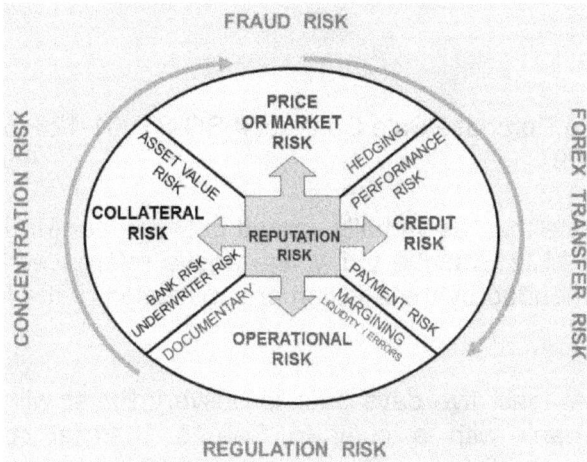

Wei Ming's Fax to SimpleTrade:

ShamOil Supply & Trading UK Ltd
Wigmore Street
London
United Kingdom
1990.02.13

FAX

SimpleTrade Associates SA
Geneva
Switzerland

Dear Sirs;

Reference Purchase/Sale Contract # SO-ST001-123456 Dated 1990.02.09

Please note that, as verbally agreed between our Mr J-F Piton and your M le Branché today, the above referenced contract will be amended by the addition or substitution of the following clauses:

"Credit: At least five days prior to delivery Buyer will send to Seller's bank with a copy to Seller's financial contact a Purchase Confirmation/Payment Undertaking in a format acceptable to Seller (bank and text will be provided)."

and

"Assignment: This agreement will not be assignable by either party without the written consent of the other, which shall not be unreasonably withheld. However, in the event payment is not made by the Buyer on due date, Seller has the right to assign the financial rights under this agreement to a bank without the prior consent of the Buyer."

You will receive a formal contract amendment from our Contracts Team later today.

An explanatory note regarding the Payment Undertaking process is included with this fax.

Yours faithfully

Lee, Wei Ming
Collateral Manager

J E Cricket
Credit Manager
Europe Middle East Africa

The Payment Undertaking Alternative to Traditional Payment Risk Security Instruments

The Payment Undertaking based arrangement described in these notes offers a viable and flexible **alternative** to payment security based on;
- Documentary Credits (including Standby Letters of Credit),
- Domestic Bank Guarantees and
- Promissory Notes

Payment Undertakings are also sometimes called Purchase Confirmations. They ask no more of the Buyer than a simple but separate confirmation that the Buyer will fulfil the terms of the contract with the Seller. A Payment Undertaking does not impose any additional burden upon the Buyer over and above that already agreed in the purchase/sale contract. It is however a separate formal irrevocable document, usually addressed directly to the bank designated by the Seller.
In preparation for this type of arrangement the relevant purchase/sale contract must contain the following two clauses:

"Credit: At least five days prior to delivery Buyer will send to Seller's bank with a copy to Seller's financial contact a Purchase Confirmation/Payment Undertaking in a format acceptable to Seller (bank and text will be provided)." and

"Assignment: This agreement will not be assignable by either party without the written consent of the other, which shall not be unreasonably withheld. However, in the event payment is not made by the Buyer on due date, Seller has the right to assign the financial rights under this agreement to a bank without the prior consent of the Buyer."

Historical Development of Payment Undertakings:

Businesses which specialise in commodity trading (Traders) usually have a limited financial asset or capital base because their main assets exist in the skills and contacts of their Executives. They therefore have difficulty establishing Documentary Credit facilities with international banks.

When such Traders participate in "back-to-back" deals in which, for example, they buy a cargo of crude oil from a National Producer, which requires all Buyers to provide Documentary Credit (LC) payment security, and sell the same cargo to a highly credit worthy oil company (Major) which does not normally provide an LC to cover its purchases, a mechanism is needed to enable an international bank to provide the Trader's LC.

Some international banks found a way to do this using Payment Undertakings. In so doing they assist in the expansion of international trade and in the safe expansion of their own business activity.

....

These banks require the Trader to arrange for the Major to issue a Payment Undertaking direct to the bank, irrevocably undertaking to pay for the cargo, **if** it is delivered as agreed in a referenced purchase/sale contract, and to route the payment directly to the account of the Trader at that specific bank; **provided** the Trader's invoice contains details of that specific bank.

This permits such banks to open LCs that they could not open otherwise, by converting client risk into documentary risk. In other words the bank controls the documents of title and the payment flows by controlling both their client's - Trader's – LC in favour of the Producer and the receipt of funds from the ultimate buyer.

This simple device enables such banks to control the receipt of the funds from the Major and payment to the Seller (National Producer) out of those same funds. Receipt of the documents of title is assured under the 'linked' LC. Receipt of the Major's payment is assured under the Payment Undertaking by provision of those documents, together with the Trader's invoice, to the Major.

In recent times the function of the Payment Undertaking has been expanded to provide an alternative method of covering general payment risk. It has proved popular in Africa, the Middle East and Asia as an alternative which is more flexible and cost effective than the use of either Documentary Credits or Domestic Bank Guarantees or Promissory Notes.

This alternative method is described below.

Utilising Payment Undertakings as a Foundation for an Alternative Form of Payment Security:

Payment Undertakings have come to be used more generally, in the international commodity trading arena, following a search for an alternative to the traditional forms of Payment Risk security/collateral because these traditional forms suffer from the following drawbacks:

Domestic Bank Guarantees:
Domestic banks tend to levy high charges for the opening of Guarantees.
Sometimes such Guarantees have to be counter-guaranteed by a non-domestic bank which raises an additional charge based on the financial standing of the opening bank, not on the **financial standing of the Buyer.**
Opening a Guarantee utilises an equivalent amount of the Buyer's line of credit with its domestic bank until the Guarantee is drawn or expires. On the other hand the Buyer may be

required to deposit cash collateral with the domestic bank until the Guarantee is drawn or expires; thus freezing valuable working capital.

They are inflexible in that it is difficult for the Buyer to arrange a partial Guarantee in cases where the Seller is prepared to carry a share of the payment risk in a single transaction on open account; that is unsecured.

Guarantees opened by domestic banks do not allow non-domestic banks an opportunity to take direct risk in the name of the Buyer.

....

Documentary Credits or Transactional Letters of Credit (LCs):

Domestic banks tend to levy high charges for the opening of LCs.

Sometimes such LCs have to be confirmed by a non-domestic bank which raises an additional charge based on the financial standing of the opening bank not on the financial standing of the Buyer.

Opening an LC utilises an equivalent amount of the Buyer's line of credit with its domestic bank, until the LC is drawn or expires. In addition the Buyer may be required to deposit cash collateral with the domestic bank until the LC is drawn or expires.

In cases where the Seller is prepared to carry a share of the payment risk in a single transaction, it may be difficult for the Buyer to arrange a Documentary LC to cover only part of a shipment.

LCs opened by domestic banks do not allow non-domestic banks an opportunity to take direct risk in the name of the Buyer.

Processing LCs imposes a heavy administrative burden on the Buyer and the Seller.

Promissory Notes:

A Promissory Note (PN) creates an obligation entirely separate from the underlying purchase/sale contract. In order to create payment security before delivery a PN based on an estimated quantity and an estimated due date must be obtained. This

90

would enable a dishonest Seller to demand payment even in the event that delivery does not take place. Therefore a significant element of trust is required on the part of the Buyer.

The Payment Undertaking alternative attempts to overcome all these drawbacks by providing the following features:
- Unlimited unsecured credit terms for the Buyer.
- No costs to the Buyer for providing payment security.
- The Buyer's traditional lines of credit are not restricted.
- Lower transaction costs achieved overall since 'intermediary bank risk' costs and 'intermediary bank handling' fees are avoided. The savings can be shared by Buyer and Seller.
- Full flexibility for the Seller to carry all or share part of the Buyer payment risk, transaction by transaction
- A recognised and legally binding undertaking which is directly linked to a specific and identifiable contract
- Only limited administration effort is required of the Buyer. This alternative means a lot less work than either an LC or Guarantee would mean for the Buyer.
- Full flexibility for the Seller to manage its country risk exposures independently of its buyer commercial risks. That is to say, if a Buyer is thought to be credit worthy in respect of a particular transaction but the aggregate exposure of transactions with other Buyers in a particular country exceeds the Seller's country limit, the excess risk can be covered without the need to involve the Buyer. All the credit worthy Buyers in the country in question continue to enjoy unsecured credit terms; while the Seller is able to utilise the Payment Undertaking(s) of one or more Buyer(s) to cover its excess country risk with a bank.

Negative Points:

The Payment Undertaking alternative requires the Buyer to be involved in some additional administrative procedures viz:
- Firstly in issuing the Payment Undertaking itself, and
- secondly in having the Payment Undertaking signatures authenticated by its own bank

Positive Points:

- The Seller can fully and flexibly use its line of credit for the Buyer to average downwards the cost of payment risk cover for each transaction. This is particularly relevant when the Seller's risk appetite does not cover the full cost of a single transaction.
- The Buyer's profile is raised amongst international banks as consideration is given at Credit Committee and Senior Executive level to the Seller's request that the banks take on the commercial risk of the Buyer directly.
- The Buyer's reputation is enhanced by building up a history of prompt payments with international banks.
- The Buyer has an option to approach participating banks later; that is when it wants to extend its range of facilities beyond those available from domestic banks.
- The Buyer can share in the savings accruing from the reduced overall cost of payment risk cover.

ooO0Ooo

....

PAGE 5 of 5

PAYMENT UNDERTAKING FORMAT

QUOTE

Date: --- DATE ---

To: ---A-BANK--- ---A-COUNTRY---
Fax Number: ---123456--- **OR** --- ADDRESS ---
Attention: ---MRS-ACCOUNT-MANAGER---
Copy: ---YOUR COMPANY/THE SELLER---
Fax Number: --- 654321 / 254367 ---
Attention: ---MR-CREDIT-ANALYST---

Message Number: ---3456XYZ78---
SUBJECT: PAYMENT UNDERTAKING

We, ---ANOTHER-COMPANY--- (hereinafter called '---ANOTHER---' and/or 'Buyer'), hereby confirm that we have

agreed to purchase from ---YOUR-COMPANY--- (hereinafter called 'Seller') approximately ---AGREED-QUANTITY--- of ---AGREED-GOODS--- at a price to be calculated as below for delivery commencing during ---AGREED-TIME-PERIOD---.
The price calculation in ---AGREED-CURRENCY--- per ---AGREED-PRICE--- **OR** ---AGREED-PRICE-FORMULA---
Settlement of the price for delivery of ---AGREED-GOODS--- to ---AGREED-DESTINATION--- (to be finalised by ---AGREED-DATE--- in accordance with the contract).
All as per contract dated ---CONTRACT-DATE--- and subsequent amendments, if any.
Buyer Reference ---789012---
Seller Reference ---987654---
Subject to performance by the Seller, we ---ANOTHER--- hereby irrevocably and unconditionally confirm that we will pay the full invoice amount without any set-off, deduction or counter claim as designated in Seller's commercial invoice to the account of ---A-BANK--- at ---ANOTHER-BANK--- in ---AGREED-COUNTRY--- account number ---456789---, on the due date per the contract being not later than ---AGREED-DAYS--- after the delivery date (delivery date equals day zero), against presentation of Seller's commercial invoice and the proof of delivery ---(COPY BILL OF LADING FOR EXAMPLE)---

This undertaking is to be construed in accordance with English law with exclusive jurisdiction in the Courts of England.

Signed by:

Name: _____

Title: _____

Authorised Signatory for:
---ANOTHER-COMPANY---
---ANOTHER-COUNTRY---.

END QUOTE

Single Risk Credit Insurance Presentation
GCMG Conference Dublin – February 1990

Single and Medium Term Credit Risks Should be Considered

A good Broker or Insurer will not try to sell a 'whole turnover' policy to a company that does not need one

Companies considering Credit and/or Political Risk Insurance (PRI) should not regard insurers as 'Lenders of Last Resort'

....

Possible Cover Categories to Consider

Short and Medium Term Commercial Cover

- Up to five year's coverage for the 'right' risk with the 'right' structure

- Insolvency only cover

- Comprehensive cover

- Non-payment risk cover

....

The Right Structure

Short Term Commercial or Comprehensive Risks

- Applies the same assessment process as 'Whole Turnover' offers
    - o Main criteria is credit worthiness of the Debtor Counterparty

Medium Term Commercial or Comprehensive Risks

- o Upfront payment of 10% to 20% usually required of the Debtor

- o Staged monthly or quarterly repayments

- o   Security/Collateral to be provided by the Debtor

- o   Insured (Creditor) should retain a greater share of the risk

- o   A Creditor-Insurer Partnership approach is essential

....

The Partnership Approach – Helping Oneself by Helping the Insurer

Challenging Risks require a Collegiate Approach

Provide the following to the Insurer:

- Debtor's recent financial statements

- Proposed sale/purchase contract structure

- Background to negotiations

- Commercial considerations that make the proposed transaction attractive

- Prospects for on-going or repeat business in future

- Past experience with the Buyer and the Buyer's Country

Specialist Insurers

- Provide small, dedicated teams

- Are not process driven

- The Insurer is in fact underwriting the Insured's confidence in the probability that the transaction will be successfully concluded.

Here Jenny had appended the following notes:

However several insurance underwriters, particularly lead Underwriters, are employing credit risk assessor teams to undertake independent in-house risk assessment of counterparties and countries. This has become essential since, in the case of single name underwriting, the Insurer is not able to rely on the portfolio effect present in respect of traditional insurance products. In the case of property damage insurance, for example, the insurer will cover a range of parties and facilities collecting a relatively small premium from each. Since it is not possible to know in advance which policy will be paid but possible to estimate the portion of the portfolio that will submit a claim, the premiums charged can be fairly accurately calculated in advance, allowing for a net return to be earned on the portfolio. On the other hand the Insured are willing to contribute towards the pool of funds to be used to pay claims since they cannot know whether they themselves will submit a claim or not. However they realise that if they unfortunately have to submit a claim it could be for the full replacement cost of their property.

Conversely in respect of a Whole Turnover Credit Insurance policy, an Insured is very reluctant to pay premiums to cover receivable invoices due from those of its clients it judges to be unlikely to fail to pay. Hence the trend towards sharing counterparty credit risk with banks or insurers on a case by case basis, when the whole notional risk in a single case is considered to be in excess of the corporate company's appetite.

....

Policy Purchasing Tips

Policy clauses can be negotiated and amended within reason

Always read the whole policy carefully

- This sounds obvious but could save distress later.

Pay extra careful attention to:

- Exclusions, Warranties and General Conditions

Credit and PRI Policies are 'living' policies

- Communication between the Insured and Insurer is key to making a policy work effectively. Full and timely disclosure of any pertinent facts or occurrences is a basic requirement.

- An Insurance Policy is a conditional contract – all stipulated conditions must be met before payment of any claim will materialise

- Compliance with all conditions throughout the currency of the policy is therefore essential

....

Duration of Single Risk Cover

Policies can be written to cover all qualifying transactions that are accepted by the Underwriter during the period of existence of the policy, up to the maximum aggregate amount allowed – usually subject to a maximum of 90% of any one transaction.

The Underwriter cannot withdraw this commitment to cover, provided the terms of the policy contract are not breached and/or no pre-defined termination event occurs.

A sales campaign and/or a term contract can therefore be arranged in the confident knowledge that the credit risk will be managed (shared) as required by corporate policy.

....

The Cost of Single Risk Insurance

The premium to be paid will usually relate closely to the unfunded risk charge levied by Banks, in respect of silent cover provided for the same or similar assessed risk.

However, note that Insurance Underwriters usually require an advance 'Deposit Premium' to be paid, as well as a 'Minimum Premium' to be paid over the life of the policy. These amounts are negotiable.

Nevertheless in a commercial context it is necessary to establish that the Deposit and/or Minimum premiums do not exceed the premium the company anticipates paying, based on forecast or contracted sales volumes.

Proposed Amended Clauses
for Risk Sharing Guarantee

Claim Amount means the Guaranteed Percentage of the Loss Amount.

Guaranteed Percentage means the percentage of each and every Loss Amount which is to be indemnified under this guarantee.

Loss means the failure of the Buyer to honour its obligations of payment to ShamOil on the relevant Due Date(s).

Loss Amount means the amount of principal (and interest if applicable) due on the Due Date and unpaid at the end of the Waiting Period in respect of the relevant invoice less:

1. Any amount received by ShamOil from any source on account of the Loss;
2. Any amount which the Buyer is entitled to credit to its own account by way of set-off or counter-claim against ShamOil;
3. Any amount which ShamOil is entitled to appropriate as, or towards, payment of the Loss Amount; and subject always to the Maximum Limit of Liability.

Waiting Period means 90 (ninety) days which must elapse from the Date of Loss - being 30 days after the relevant NOR date - before any claim is payable under this guarantee.

Notice of Loss: ShamOil will give written notice to the Bank within 30 (thirty) days of becoming aware of a circumstance which could result in a Loss.

Application of Funds

For the purposes of determining the Bank's liability under this guarantee:

1. All funds received by ShamOil after the Buyer is in default of its obligations under an invoice shall first be

applied to overdue principal and interest accrued up to the Due Date.

2. If ShamOil receives funds from the Buyer after such default, that are not specifically attributable to the invoice in question or any other particular outstanding debt, then such sum shall be applied first to the oldest outstanding debt whether guaranteed hereunder or not.

3. No funds shall be applied to interest accruing after the default (including but not limited to penalty interest) until the outstanding overdue principal and interest accrued up to the date of default is paid in full.

4. ShamOil agrees to allow the Bank full access to whatever information and documents it may possess which could assist the Bank in reviewing the way in which the funds have been applied.

Co-operation with the Bank

ShamOil shall co-operate fully with the Bank in the investigation of any claim and the pursuit of any claim recovery. Such co-operation shall include disclosure of records and documents and the making available of witnesses as well as providing assistance to any other party appointed by the Bank to investigate ShamOil's claim.

Due Diligence

ShamOil will at all times use due diligence and do, and concur in doing, and permit to be done, all things reasonably practicable at its own expense to avoid any Loss or minimise any Loss Amount.

Loss minimisation

Prior to any claim payment, ShamOil will at ShamOil's cost pursue all reasonable diplomatic, legal, administrative, judicial and informal means which may be reasonably available for the minimisation or recovery of any Loss. ShamOil shall take all steps and action to affect recoveries, whether from the Buyer, a guarantor or from any other party from whom such recoveries may be made. Such steps may include the institution of proceedings or the appointment of an agent or attorney of ShamOil, subject to the written approval of the Bank, for the purpose of collecting recoveries. The costs of complying with this Condition shall be borne by ShamOil before payment of a claim and **after payment of a claim shall be shared between the Bank and ShamOil in accordance with the relative proportions that the Claim Amount bears to the Loss Amount.**

Assignment and Subrogation

At the time of payment of any Claim Amount under this guarantee the Bank shall be subrogated to, and if the Bank requests ShamOil shall assign to the Bank, all ShamOil's rights of recovery against the Buyer and/or any other party, and ShamOil shall execute and deliver all instruments and papers to the Bank and do whatever else is necessary to secure such rights. ShamOil shall do nothing to prejudice such rights. If the Bank requests assignment, all such assignment(s) shall be free and clear of claims, defences, counterclaims, rights of set off and other encumbrances.

Recoveries

After payment of any Claim Amount hereunder any sums related to the unpaid invoice which are recovered from any source, less the costs of recovery thereof shall be **shared between the Bank and ShamOil in accordance with the relative proportions that the Claim Amount bears to the Loss Amount.** ShamOil acknowledges that any sums which it obtains by way of recovery due to the Bank hereunder, it shall hold on trust for the Bank. Any sums received from the Buyer, which are not specifically attributable to any particular outstanding debt under the Contract, shall be shared between the Bank and ShamOil in proportion to insured and uninsured losses under the Contract.

Bibliography

Berlin Wall
http://www.history.com/topics/berlin-wall
The Berlin Wall: The Fall of the Wall
http://www.history.com/topics/berlin-wall#a4

The Black Swan: The Impact of the Highly Improbable by
Nassim Nicholas Taleb

Leading the Revolution: How to Thrive in Turbulent Times by
Making Innovation a Way of Life by Gary Hamel

New Barbarian Manifesto by Ian Angell

Origins of the Battle of Blood River 1838
The Great Trek and the advent of the Mfecane
The various versions of the death of Piet Retief
Dingane raises Port Natal to the ground
http://www.sahistory.org.za/origins-battle-blood-river-1838

Battle of Blood River 1838
http://www.sahistory.org.za/south-africa-1806-1899/battle-
blood-river-1838

FW de Klerk: The day I ended apartheid.
Article carried by The Independent on February 2, 2010, see:
http://www.independent.co.uk

Britannica Online Encyclopaedia
http://www.britannica.com/EBchecked/topic/153615/FW-de-
Klerk

FW de Klerk Foundation – Centre for Constitutional Rights
http://www.fwdklerk.org.za

Czechoslovakia
http://www.spartacus.schoolnet.co.uk/2WWczech.htm

40 years on: the exile comes home to Prague

http://www.guardian.co.uk/artanddesign/2008/aug/24/photography

Synagogue.cz
http://www.synagogue.cz/jewish-monumets/synagogues/the-old-new-synagogue-2/

Reduta Jazz Club in Prague
http://www.pragueexperience.com

The Focus Collection – Hans Dulfer
http://www.focuscollection.com/homepages/h0025.html

Kees Hazevoet: Interview by Clifford Allen
http://www.paristransatlantic.com/magazine/interviews/hazevoet.html

British Embassy in Prague website
ukinczechrepublic.fco.gov.uk/

Foreign Office Files: United States of America
Series Three: The Cold War
Public Record Office Class FO 371 and Related Files
Part 2: The Prague Spring and Soviet Intervention in
Czechoslovakia, 1967-1968
http://www.ampltd.co.uk/digital_guides/fo_usa_series_3_part_2/publishers-note.aspx

Warsaw Pact Invasion of Czechoslovakia
http://en.wikipedia.org/wiki/Warsaw_Pact_invasion_of_Czechoslovakia

Negotiating with the Soviets by Raymond F. Smith

Treaty on the Final Settlement with Respect to Germany -
Wikipedia
See: http://en.wikipedia.org

Germany's Unlikely Diplomatic Triumph: An Inside Look at the Reunification Negotiations
by Klaus Wiegrefe
http://www.spiegel.de/international/germany/germany-s-unlikely-diplomatic-triumph-an-inside-look-at-the-reunification-negotiations-a-719848-6.html

U.S. Department of State – Office of the Historian
Travels of Secretary of State James Addison Baker
http://history.state.gov

Timur Stepanov (re Shevardnadze), 1990
Interview with Timur Stepanov, assistant to Eduard Shevardnadze
Interviewer — Julia Kalinina, on behalf of Metta Spencer
Introductory notes by Julia Kalinina
http://russianpeaceanddemocracy.com/timur-stepanov-1990

Nobel Lecture – June 5, 1991
Mikhail Gorbachev – 1990 Peace Prize Laureate
http://www.nobelprize.org

Single Risk Credit Insurance
A presentation by Fergus Fergusson given at the FCIB Conference in Athens, February 2005

Global Credit Management – an Executive Summary
by Ron Wells
http://www.barrettwells.com/gcm.html

Other Credit Risk Management Research
http://www.barrettwells.co.uk and http://www.barrettwells.com

OTHER PUBLISHED BOOKS BY THIS AUTHOR:

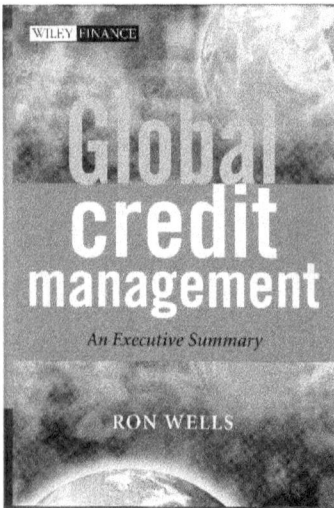

唤醒平衡表上的睡狮
国际信用管理实用指南

ISBN: 978-0-470-85111-1   ISBN: 978-988-99586-1-9

Both books are available through
http://www.t3plimited.com/estore.html